FOREIGN GOODS

GOODS

edited by JINGAN YOUNG

A
Selection
of Writing
by British
East Asian
Artists

FOREIGN GOODS:
A Selection of Writing
by British East Asian Artists

edited by Jingan Young

OBERON BOOKS
LONDON

WWW.OBERONBOOKS.COM

First published in 2018 by Oberon Books Ltd
521 Caledonian Road, London N7 9RH
Tel: +44 (0) 20 7607 3637 / Fax: +44 (0) 20 7607 3629
e-mail: info@oberonbooks.com
www.oberonbooks.com

PB ISBN: 9781786823588
E ISBN: 9781786823595

Designed by Konstantinos Vasdekis

Printed and bound by 4EDGE Limited, Hockley, Essex, UK.
eBook conversion by Lapiz Digital Services, India.

Visit www.oberonbooks.com to read more about all our books and to buy them.
You will also find features, author interviews and news of any author events, and
you can sign up for e-newsletters so that you're always first to hear about our new
releases.

Printed on FSC accredited paper

Contents

FOREWORD
by Jingan Young

I first discovered the phrase 'Foreign Goods Last Forever' within an essay written by my father John Dragon Young in the year he died entitled, 'Thanks for the Memories (1996)'. The work appeared in 'City Voices', a 2003 collection of Hong Kong writing in English. It was his mother's favourite phrase, and referred to the donations of food and goods provided by the US Army and the Red Cross during the time they lived as impoverished Chinese refugees in Diamond Hill during the 1950s.

Although my grandmother was referring to the imported 'chocolates, chewing gum, beans, blankets and beds', to me, the expression symbolises the convergence of East and West. It reflects my upbringing in Hong Kong, a city of multilingual voices and multicultural communities and my decision to move to Britain in 2009 to study and pursue a career as a writer. Born in Hong Kong before the 1997 Handover, my childhood memories contain a mixture of red UK Royal Mail post boxes, re-runs of *Judge John Deed* on television, Dim-Sum Sundays, visits to the Forbidden City and my mother treating me to special shopping trips to M&S. This phrase, embedded in the work by a man I hardly knew, appears to echo my own ongoing attempt to reconcile my third culture identity. In one sense, it signifies a relationship I will never have with my father as an adult. It seemed apt that I would apply this as the moniker for an ongoing theatrical showcase for British East Asian writers that I have produced with my company Pokfulam Rd Productions since 2016.

Since its inaugural 'guerrilla' production at Theatre503, the 'Foreign Goods' showcases have proven not only popular amongst those in the industry and local East Asian communities but have also attracted those who have never seen contemporary East Asian stories on UK stages. The latter is an ongoing problem. Despite the existence of more than three BEA theatre companies in London, there is a real dearth of awareness for their work and often, knowledge of their existence. Why, if we are living in a society which exhaustively celebrates diversity, are BEAs still so often marginalised and ignored? This vicious cycle obstructs both the artist and the future artist. For why would a young BEA pursue a career in an industry which does not recognise them?

This collection of eight plays is our attempt to change the conversation.

Together with the supportive collaboration of Oberon Books we present 8 stories written by playwrights of East and South-East Asian descent. There are stories on the unreliable nature of memory, the politics of aging, poetic imaginings of the migrant's journey, conflicts in defining your sexuality, humorous cross-cultural tales as told by an aspiring actor, the housing crisis, and confessing your Western fetish...

Shortly after discussions early on with Oberon editor Lucy Smith we ultimately came to the consensus that this collection would exist as a sort of toolkit. Containing full-length plays, short plays and monologues, this collection exists to provide a plethora of opportunity, as audition material for young actors, full and short-length pieces for burgeoning companies, a book for the curious and to enlighten those interested or ignorant of British East Asian culture.

This is the first ever collection of British East Asian plays published in the United Kingdom. I very much hope you enjoy reading them.

Special Thanks

Firstly, I must thank the writers of this first collection: Amber Hsu, Cathy Lam, Kathryn Golding, Julie Cheung-Inhin, Lucy Sheen, Stephen Hoo and Suet Tan. Your stories are unique, relatable, unbounded by clichés, and fearless in their resistance to stereotypical East Asian representation. Your work speaks to everyone and it is an honour to include them in this seminal step for British East Asian artists.

I must also thank those writers who have participated in past 'Foreign Goods' showcases: Amal Chatterjee, Naomi Sumner, Naomi Christie and Amy Ng whose play has gone on to have a full production at Hampstead Theatre Downstairs! I have no doubt that these writers will very soon become household names.

Thank you to producer Jessica Campbell, Theatre503's literary manager Steve Harper, artistic director Lisa Spirling and the rest of the 503 team for supporting the 'Foreign Goods' showcase from the beginning, allowing us to stage these plays at their gem in Battersea from 2016 – 2017.

Great thanks are owed to Tom Wright, Old Vic New Voices and Freya Aitken-Turff and Helena Zhang of the China Exchange for generously providing rehearsal space often at a moment's notice and at no cost.

I must express overwhelming gratitude to all creative teams for Foreign Goods 1 & 2 and in no particular order: Lucy Roslyn, Ben Norris, Shenagh Govan, Angela Harvey, Eugenia Low, Holly Fry, Kit Lloyd, David East, Christina May, Hilary Harwood, Charlotte Chiew (Foreign Goods One), Shuang Teng, Brian Law, Windson Liong, Velda Hassan, Danny Steele, Chris Keyna, Kate Llewellyn, Gilbert Kyem, Waylon Ma, Matthew Houston, Chloe Ewert and Michael Phong Le (Foreign Goods Two). Directors Alice Kornitzer, Beth Kapila, Grace Joseph, Mingyu Lin, Max Lindsay, Kim Pearce, Tessa Hart and Ian Nicholson. Without you, these plays would have had no life. You gave them a heartbeat. If only there was room to list the creatives for our third showcase which will take place shortly after this collection is published!

I must thank Max Percy who worked as my co-producer on our ambitious second and third outing of Foreign Goods. Max is unwavering in his dedication and enthusiasm for the project. He is an unstoppable force.

The journey from stage to page has been a long one. Thank you to Emma Hall and Tia Begum for opening up the first conversation with Oberon Books. I am indebted to Lucy Smith for continuing to see the potential and importance of the collection. Lucy has been unwavering in her honesty, support and dedication every step of the way towards its publication. Thank you to the rest of the team at Oberon Books, including Wei Ming Kam and Aine Ryan, George Spender and designer Konstantinos Vasdekis who produced a wonderfully vibrant and striking book design (thank you especially for never mentioning the word 'dragon' in our discussions!)

I personally must pay my respects to the *Soy Sauce* team: producer Clarissa Widya of Papergang Theatre, director Freyja Winterson, designer, stage manager and man-of-all-trades Archie Macleod, actors Alex Wilson, Robert Bradley and Joyce Veheary for developing, performing and producing this play throughout its 2016 London tour. I must also thank the Camden People's Theatre, Illuminate Festival and Stewart Pringle whilst he was artistic director of the Old Red Lion, Pippa Howie for assisting in workshopping its first reading with actors Jason Rosenthal and Anna Leong Brophy. For Julie Cheung-Inhin, Jamie Giles and Rikki Beadle Blair for developing and showing an excerpt of the play in 2017.

Much thanks must also be given to those who attended the Foreign Goods showcases over the years. Without you, this collection would not have existed.

Thank you to David Henry Hwang for acting as a constant source of inspiration, as mentor and for the beautiful accompanying foreword to this collection.

Lastly, to my mother Kerrie, my closest friends and my partner Slane for their love and support.

FOREWORD
by David Henry Hwang

Back in the late 1970s, as a student in the San Francisco Bay Area, I discovered a small but growing group of artists creating a vital new form: Asian American Theatre. Having grown up virtually invisible in mainstream American culture, save for occasional appearances as the villainous male, exoticised female, or butt of racist jokes, Asian Americans began to create works neither white American nor root-culture Asian, bringing our unique stories and perspectives to fully human life. Decades later, I asked the acclaimed Japanese American dramatist Philip Kan Gotanda, 'Of all that's happened over the years, what would you never have predicted back when we were starting out?' He replied, 'I never thought we would be studied or published.'

Though plays are written to be performed, publication endows this most ephemeral of art forms with some degree of permanence. Moreover, printing expands a work's audiences, encourages future productions, and acknowledges its literary worth. This publication of *Foreign Goods: A Selection of Writing by British East Asian Artists* therefore stands as an important event in the exciting and rapidly-growing British East Asian theatre movement. As an Asian American artist, I like to think we enjoy a 'special relationship' with our counterparts across the pond. Though we share many of the same joys and challenges, however, the plays in this volume shine with experiences and viewpoints which are uniquely BEA. Consider the discussion of 'What makes Great Britain great?' in *I'm Just Here to Buy Soy Sauce*. Or 'Paki' as a racial taunt in *Suzy Wong: Fitting In and Fucking Up* or the widow denied a war pension because her husband wasn't white in *Under a Blood Red Moon*. As always, the cultural specificity of these works infuses them with universality.

Good theatre allows us to simultaneously perceive both superficial differences and the underlying humanity we share. In a world where nations grow increasingly interdependent, as we live in countries whose continued vitality depends on the infusion of new immigrants and cultural perspectives, these plays deserve to be read, performed and studied. They celebrate the arrival and promise of a vital new form: British East Asian Theatre.

NO MORE LOTUS FLOWER!
by JULIE CHEUNG-INHIN

Production History

No More Lotus Flower! was first performed at the Camden People's Theatre as part of Camden Fringe on the 26th August 2015 with the following cast and creative team:

Cast
Julie Cheung-Inhin

Creative Team
Writer	Julie Cheung-Inhin
Director and Dramaturg	Lavinia Hollands
Lighting Designer	David Meunier-Palmer
Stage Manager	Ria Samartzi

As a general note throughout the play, lines in bold indicate a character that JULIE is portraying (which can also be herself), lines not in bold <u>always</u> indicate a NEUTRAL JULIE who addresses the audience directly.

The stage has a chair USL to the right of which is a small table. DSR is a red box which includes various props that one might use to play 'East Asian' dress-up, e.g. a kimono, a pair of chopsticks, and an Asian tea set, as well as props one might use to play 'white' dress-up, e.g. a blonde wig, an English cup and saucer, and pink lipstick.

As the opening voiceover says, 'How much Chinese do you know?' JULIE enters with a bag of props that will be used throughout the play. These can of course be tailored to each specific production and how one wishes to portray the various characters. Those listed here are suggestions which were used in the original production: a pair of reading glasses attached to a neck cord, a baseball cap, a modern pair of glasses, a mobile phone, and a folder inside of which is a headshot of an East Asian woman. JULIE stands centre and reacts to the voiceover.

VOICEOVER: Do you speak Chinese?

VOICEOVER (JULIE): No.

VOICEOVER: You don't speak Chinese?!

VOICEOVER (JULIE): No.

VOICEOVER: How much Chinese do you know?

VOICEOVER (JULIE): None. A few swear words, maybe?

The following takes place in the style of a PowerPoint presentation with slides, PRESENTATION JULIE directly addresses her audience. If there is no projector available, images in a folder or flipchart can be used instead.

PRESENTATION JULIE: Let's start with the basics, shall we? You're probably wondering where I'm from. *(Beat.)* Where I'm *really* from.

I was born here, but my parents were born in Mauritius *(Slide 1: map of Mauritius)*. That's Mauritius. Not Malaysia. *(Slide 2: map of Malaysia crossed out)* Mauritius *(Slide 3: map of Mauritius)*.

Beat.

Oh, but my grandparents were from China *(Slide 4: the word 'China' in large red letters)*, that's why. Indeed, you do get Chinese people from Mauritius. It's a multi-cultural country.

Of course, I do consider myself East Asian, being ethnically Chinese. East Asia *(Slide 5: map of East Asia, which has the following country names pop us as they are mentioned)* usually refers to China, Japan, North Korea, South Korea, Mongolia and Taiwan, but it can also include places in Southeast Asia, such as Myanmar, Laos, Vietnam, Thailand, Cambodia, the Philippines, Malaysia, Singapore, and Indonesia.

Oh and I speak Creole *(Slide 6: the word 'Creole')*, which is a bit like French but without the grammar *('French without the grammar' pops up on the slide)*.

Any questions?

Great! Now that I've got that out of the way, I can get on with the show!

(Empties bag of props onto the table during the following.) Hi, I'm Julie, and I'm an actor.

It was F. Scott Fitzgerald who said you don't write because you want to say something, you write because you have something to say.

Basically, something happened to me as I was leaving drama school, and it made me think I should write about it.

PRINCIPAL: *(Puts on reading glasses and stands on the chair, note the glasses can hang around the neck throughout the show when not acting as the PRINCIPAL.)* Now then, this is just a notice for all final year students. As you know, all drama schools are invited to put forward up to four students for the BBC radio competition known as the Carleton Hobbs. The winning students are offered a five month contract with the BBC. In order to choose which students to put forward, we're going to hold in-house auditions. All students are welcome to audition, so long as you are able to speak in a standard English accent.

Spots JULIE DSR, jumps off chair to catch up to her.

Ah, Julie!

I just wanted a quick word. I noticed that you had signed up for the Carleton Hobbs auditions.

Yes, about that... I just wanted to ask you whether you would be comfortable speaking in a standard English accent.

I mean, your speech tutor may have told you that your natural accent is standard English, but...well, it's just that I wanted people to know that we *will* be holding separate auditions like this for people with foreign accents so that there's no need to audition for the Carleton Hobbs. Obviously these will be mock auditions and not for a real competition like Carleton Hobbs but we want people to know that they can still have a go at auditioning. So you don't have to feel left out.

Pause.

But, not to worry, if you think you'll be able to speak in a standard English accent that should be fine.

(Move to DS centre, removing glasses.) Well...it was odd. I was born in London and I'd lived here my whole life, so, yes, I was comfortable speaking in a standard English accent.

Also, not only had my speech tutor said that my natural accent was standard English, but it was generally known amongst my peers that I was one of the closest to having an RP accent in my year... So much so that my voice teacher had suggested to some of our international students that, if they wanted to hear an RP accent, they should listen to mine...

And you know, he'd seen all the performances I'd done in over a year and a half of training, so he ought to have known this. I mean, I did actually have lines. People did hear me speak.

Finally, there were a number of other students in my year from around the UK with regional accents to match. He didn't ask *them* if they were comfortable speaking in a standard English accent. Were they white? *(Knowing look to audience to demonstrate that, 'Yes, they were')*.

PRINCIPAL: It's just that, Julie, sometimes when you speak I detect a slight American accent or something. But, like I said, what matters is if you're able to speak in standard English accent – it should be fine.

I mulled over this before coming to two possible explanations.

Wears the baseball cap for LA SHOP ASSISTANT, when being JULIE moves to stand opposite the chair and removes the cap.

LA SHOP ASSISTANT: *(In an American accent.)* Hey! Welcome to LA! So where are you from?

JULIE: Hi! Thank you! I'm from London. I've never been to America before – this is most exciting.

LA SHOP ASSISTANT: That is so cool. I've been to London once – Heathrow, man! I love that airport – it was so huge!

JULIE: Haha, mm. Yes, it is quite a big hub.

LA SHOP ASSISTANT: Yeah, yeah. *(Beat.)* God, it's so weird – you're Asian, but you have this really cool British accent!

JULIE: *(Laughs.)* Well, you're Asian too and you have an American accent! It's kind of the same thing, right?

Okay, so my one week in LA probably didn't affect my accent and give me an American twang. *(Pause.)* Perhaps it was this instead?

Discards the baseball cap, takes the modern glasses and wears them as VANESSA. Removes the glasses to become JULIE.

VANESSA: Hey there! I'm Vanessa! So, is this your first day?

JULIE: Hi! I'm Julie! No, I'm actually a second year! *(To audience.)* She's East Asian! Of course, I'm British, so I don't just go up to another Asian and ask them about their background... But I do want to know...! *(Turns back to look at VANESSA, awkward pause.)*

VANESSA: So you're British? I'm from Singapore.

JULIE: Cool! *(Looks to audience.)* I love how forward she is!

VANESSA: It's great to see I'm not the only Asian here.

JULIE: Yeah, we're like, the only two Asians in the whole school.

(Discards the modern glasses.) That's when I realised that if my Principal still gets me mixed up with the only other Asian in the whole school, I don't just want to put on this show, I *have* to put on this show.

JULIE: 'Oh spite! Oh hell!' *(Struggling.)*

I was in my voice class, practising my audition speech for the Carleton Hobbs.

JULIE: 'Ohh spite! Ohh hell!' *(And again.)* 'Oh SPITE! Oh HELL!'

VOICE TEACHER: So, you do seem to be struggling with that section. What you want to think about is bringing the breath down low. Right down here. Your pelvis. Think of your core, the birthplace of your emotions. Feel them bursting through you. *(Pause, various voice exercises, 'ha ha ha haaaa' etc, before lightbulb moment.)* Could it perhaps be because of something in your upbringing? *(Pause.)* Is there something in your culture that makes you hold things in? Perhaps when you were growing up you weren't really able to show your emotions?

I began to wonder whether my ethnicity was getting in the way. So I asked my Principal.

PRINCIPAL: Ah, Julie. You're being over-sensitive. It's like anything. I'm English and, you know, people say, ooh, football violence and we drink too much. I don't drink. I don't even like football, but, you know, *I* deal with it.

During drama school we were always told that an important part of being an actor is going out to *see* theatre. Good theatre, bad theatre – you should see as much as you can for your own personal development as an actor. I did, and still do, grab the opportunity to see as much as I can and, whilst it gives me the chance to compare and contrast what I've been taught at school with what I see on stage, I have also learnt something else.

Picks up mobile phone from the table and sits on the chair reading it while Twitter and Facebook images are projected to portray 'The Orphan of Zhao' controversy.

JULIE: *(Reading from the phone.)* **West End theatre facing criticism...**

17 strong company featuring only three actors of East Asian heritage...

...Performing *The Orphan of Zhao*, **a piece that is often referred to as the Chinese** *Hamlet*.

Set in China with Chinese characters and costumes... the only parts given to actors of East Asian heritage are two dogs. And a maidservant...who dies...

...Chinese boy on the flyer...but an almost *all white cast*.

I started to worry that this might affect my future career and decided to look for more information. I saw a clip of Daniel York discussing the situation. Daniel is an actor, and the previous Chair of Equity's Minority Ethnic Artists' Committee:

DANIEL YORK: It-it really bothers me that-that-that the term colour-blind casting's now...been appropriated and gets used...by...people to defend situations like this. I mean it happened in the *More Light* **one; I-I remember, erm, our-our-our dear friend Ian Shuttleworth...from the** *Financial Times*, **y-you know, a-a-absolutely used that one, you know, 'This is colour-blind casting, can you not see? Everyone's white. It's colour-blind casting.' Y-you know, erm, and it-it's worth remembering th-th-that colour-blind casting w-w-was a mechanism that-that, you know, was designed to create opportunities for people...from... minority backgrounds, who wouldn't otherwise have opportunities. Not to protect the privilege of the dominant social racial demographic, which is, you know, I – to me, this is rampant protectionism. Erm, it-it's not, I mean, I-I-I know – I mean I-I-I've-I've actually had a – had a – meeting with the RSC**

a-a-about this and-and-and th-they...y-you know, in-in-in a, in a way they're being very nice about it but-but-but they-they-they couldn't get their head round the fact that this is not a diverse cast.

I had also seen a play called *Yellowface* at the National Theatre which actually dealt with this issue. I decided to talk to Kevin Shen who produced the play as well as acted in it.

INTERVIEW JULIE: So, Kevin, what do you think about colour-blind casting?

KEVIN SHEN: Erm, what I think has come into play a lot that I hear, is they go, 'Oh no, we've cast it colour-blind and so we quote-on-quote ignored the race of all the actors and we've picked the quote-on-quote best actor for the part' and, er, of course, erm, you know, white male who has, er, a list of credits as long as his arm versus black male who's only played drug dealers...urm... 'white guy was just a better actor!' And I think...that is...terrible.

It seems there is such an unlevel playing field between white actors and actors of ethnic minority. Kevin mentioned black actors, but if we think the hierarchy of minorities on screen and stage goes black, South Asian, then East Asian, we get the general idea that colour-blind casting gets to a be a great reason for other actors to play...dress up as East Asians!

Picks up red box DSR, brings it to the centre and opens it to play dress up: sticks two chopsticks in her hair, puts on the kimono, takes out Asian tea set, pours tea etc.

Of course, traditionally yellowface referred to stereotypical impersonations of East Asians, by, for example, cosmetic devices or physical gestures. But it also encompasses any performance of an Asian role by a non-Asian actor, even when they are not stereotyped.

Blackface nowadays is – correctly – frowned upon. There's no way Othello would be played by a white person (unless they were making an actual statement about racism, maybe). But yellowface is apparently fine.

There are many reasons why we go to see theatre. One reason is to learn about ourselves. *The Orphan of Zhao* taught me that, while my culture is attractive, my face is not. The theatre teaches us what it means to be human. *The Orphan of Zhao* taught me I would be better casting for a dog. Gemma Chan herself plays a robot in a show called *Humans*. If theatre is a cultural space where society examines itself in a mirror, then where is my reflection as I leave drama school?

Do I belong here, as an actor, at all?

Shrugs, 'I don't know'. Removes kimono and chopsticks, places them on the chair. Then thinks, 'What if I whited up?' Gets out from the same red box a blonde wig, some make-up that a blonde girl might use e.g. pink lipstick, and an English tea set. Takes a selfie.

(*Removes wig.*) You see, you've got white actors playing Asian roles, but it's not like East Asians are allowed to play white roles, they're not even able to play roles which are open ethnicity. I have this friend, Siu-see, a Eurasian actress...

SIU-SEE HUNG: So everyone was meant to hear the next week, early, like Monday, Tuesday, and she said that she was gonna let me know either way so it was already a bit weird that I was, like – 'cause I – you know, I came out with, 'I got it.' But then, erm, when I hadn't heard by Tuesday I was like, 'Okay, well, I guess I haven't got it.' So, you know, that's how things go.

But, erm, I got an email from her saying, 'Oh, we need a few more days to decide,' so, that's never a good sign, so, whatever, I just assumed I hadn't got it by then.

And then later on that week I got an email from her saying, erm, you know, 'Thank you so much for your time, we loved your work...' erm, 'Unfortunately, this time...' er, 'you've not been chosen.' And then at that point I was like, 'Okay, fine, disappointing, but fine.' What happened – and then she carried on. She's like, 'I could not securely convince the creative team of the possibilities of the text to be discovered in a cultural...difference...background.' Some – along those lines. Th-that was pretty much, apart from the ending, a direct quote.

So I was, I dunno, I was just really, really hurt. Like, it basically sounded like if I were white I would have that part. I, like, I would have rather her say – ee – my acting wasn't good enough, someone else was better, because I can work on that. I can't work on the colour of my skin.

I forget sometimes that all too often the outside world will only see the colour of my skin which obliterates everything else. For example where I trained, or sometimes even *if* I trained...my skills... personality...

PRINCIPAL: *(To the audience.)* Now then. Soon you'll be leaving drama school for the big wide world of acting. It's important that you know what your casting type is. *(Picking out audience members for the following casting types.)* You're the alpha male, IT geek, blonde bombshell, yummy mummy, Mr Darcy, quirky sidekick, prom queen, jock... *(And so on and so forth until he spots JULIE DSR.)* Ah Julie! *(Searching, and then...)* Chinese!

Chinese is a casting type in itself?

CASTING CALL JULIE: Hi, yes, I'm here for the role of Chinese waitress.

DAVID: Hello, yes, I'm here for the role of Chinese waiter.

CASTING CALL JULIE: Oh, hi, David! Nice to see you!

A big part of being an actor is rejection. Like if an agency rejects me with (*takes out East Asian female headshot from the folder, shows to audience*) 'there are too many similarities between yourself and a client we have recently taken on.'

So I was surprised when this happened...

PRINCIPAL: (*Picks up phone.*) Hello? Yes. Okay. Oh, yes! Yes, I have an oriental student in my school, yes! Like *Crouching Tiger Hidden Dragon*? Well she's just completed her stage combat exam, I think she'll be perfect for it. I'll let her know, and then get her to call you? Excellent. (*Puts down phone.*)

(*Sees JULIE.*) Ah, Julie. I hope you're not too disappointed about the Carleton Hobbs. These things happen all the time. And, besides, there's an even better opportunity for *you*. A role has come up for a ninjutsu sword fighter. Why don't you brush up on your sword fighting and get in touch with the agent? I'll give you his number!

PRINCIPAL runs off.

Well, I guess I better practise then...!

At home, practises choreography of rapier and dagger – a very British style: e.g. advances, retreats and circular parries. Consider that this needs to be more 'Asian' and put some martial arts style music on, and the kimono. Picks up phone – or folder if there is no projector – flicks through it and shows images on screen/folder of martial arts poses. Puts phone/folder down and adopts these poses with adjustments etc. After a brief struggle with the poses, she topples over.

Having practised, I then went to meet the agent.

PROSPECTIVE AGENT: Hello Julie, please, take a seat! Welcome, welcome. So, Julie...that's not your real

name, is it? You might want to consider using your Chinese name. Just a thought.

So anyway, if you join my agency I could be putting you forward for jobs within two days. There are so many roles for you out there. I could put you up for so many things – there are lots of oriental castings which you'll be perfect for.

People are looking for orientals everywhere – you know, oriental tourist, oriental businesswoman, oriental concubine, oriental...whatever. Basically – you can do anything, anything oriental. (*Beat.*) Yes, most of them are commercials. Not so many in plays, no. I will only put you forward for oriental roles, yes. The roles which are open ethnicity? No, to be honest, I won't put you up for them, because you'll be at a disadvantage. You'll be at a disadvantage.

But cheer up! Think about what you *do* have a chance for! Foreigners, prostitutes, lotus flower. In America, you're lucky enough to have even more, over there you can also be a dragon lady, a geek and a kung fu fighter. Remember when you were at school and people asked if you could do kung fu? It was a compliment, right? So, do you have a sword fight ready to show me? (*Strikes a 'kung fu' pose.*)

Great! So after two years of intensive drama school training, things were going well. I had an agent (not that one), I was getting auditions, even callbacks...!

The following is to be enacted as a monologue with the director's voice present but not heard.

JULIE: Hello, I'm Julie Cheung-Inhin.

(*Sitting down.*) Thank you.

Thanks for seeing the audition tape, I'm glad you liked it!

The role? Okay, so it's a great East Asian role; I felt that Shenshen was very layered, from being a concubine to a prostitute and then finally a mother just before she gets killed.

(*Pause, nodding.*) Oh, Chinese traditions? Yes, I mean, well, I was born here but my parents are Mauritian – Chinese Mauritian...and my grandparents were from China, so, although I'd say I'm fairly British, I was exposed to some – a lot of – Chinese culture, yes, whilst growing up. (*Beat.*) Um, Chinese New Year...red packets... I love dim sum and jasmine tea...the number 8... Oh! One tradition we follow very closely is honouring our dead ancestors. During a trip to China my parents – I – visited a shop that sells these paper objects which are burned as offerings to the dead. Yes, there were all sorts of objects there, like shirts and cars made of paper. We burned them as offerings to my grandfather. The idea is, that in burning paper shirts, cars, money, we are giving these objects to my grandfather to use in the afterlife.

Oh! Chinese films! Well, I really liked *House of Flying Daggers*...and... *Memoirs of a Geisha*...?

Yes, so going back to the character – as Shenshen is the sixth wife of the Emperor you would expect her to have the lowest status in the household and (*an interruption*) – oh, her awareness of her femininity? I'm sorry, do you mean...? (*Beat.*) Oh, well, I see that this would perhaps affect her physicality...? Show you? Yes, of course... (*Reposition to sit demurely, legs together and to the side, hands lightly clasped.*) I can imagine she would be very elegant, and demure. (*Beat.*) Yes, her hands... (*Adopt flowing hand gestures.*) They too would be very elegant. (*Pause, then speak more softly.*) I feel her voice would be sweet, quite musical, yes. (*Pause, then speak in a Chinese accent*.) Oh, yes, I can. Well, it's a Cantonese accent I think, but, yes, Chinese.

(*Pause*.) Yes, no, the last thing she would be is confrontational so I expect she would keep her eyes down low... (*Casts eyes down*.)

No, I don't speak... (*Beat, must make something up*.) Erm...lei ho, lei ho...erm, gung hei fat choy...ho ho... pak choy...

Silk? Erm, I don't really own any silk clothing... No, not really. Well, I wear satin pyjamas to sleep. I mean, it's really pretty and comfortable.

(*Pause*.) Using a fan? Well, yes, I've had training in using a fan! This was at drama school. When we did our restoration comedy.

(*Gets up from chair*.) So it turns out I'm pretty niche. It's great. A role for 'Oriental Girl'? Oh yes! Japanese tourist? Hi! Geisha girl? Hai.

But of course, the problem is, I don't wear silk. The closest thing I have are my satin pyjamas. I'm not a graceful lotus flower. I fall over too often and I'm not quiet! But you know what else? Go to Hong Kong, Singapore, China, and you won't see people walking around in silk bowing to each other!

It's as if there's no such thing as a British East Asian. I am British. Why do I have to fight so hard to represent the nationality that I was born into?

In January 2017 a theatre in Notting Hill called The Print Room put on a play. The play was called *In the Depths of Dead Love* by Howard Barker. It was set in China and all the characters had Chinese names. All the actors were white.

The reasoning for this was because...

THE PRINT ROOM: It is, in fact a very 'English' play and is derived from thoroughly English mores and simply references the mythic and the ancient. It has therefore been cast accordingly.

In October 2017 Music Theatre Wales put on an opera. The opera was called *Golden Dragon* based on the original play by Roland Schimmelpfennig.
It was set in a Chinese restaurant with character names such as Chinese Mother, Chinese Father, Chinese Aunt, and Chinese Uncle. All the actors were white.

The reasoning for this was because...

MUSIC THEATRE WALES: The original play, and the opera on which it is based, is post-Brechtian story-telling. There is no realism.

There is no such thing as a British East Asian.

If I was white, I wouldn't have to bear this social burden of race.

VOICEOVER: Do you speak Chinese?

VOICEOVER (JULIE): No.

VOICEOVER: You don't speak Chinese?!

VOICEOVER (JULIE): No.

VOICEOVER: So how much Chinese do you know?

VOICEOVER (JULIE): None.

THE END.

Julie Cheung-Inhin is a British-born East Asian actor and writer.

In 2015 she wrote and performed her satirical solo show *No More Lotus Flower!* as part of the Camden Fringe. Her work in theatre includes: *The 38th Parallel* (Pokfulam Road Productions at the Park Theatre), *Eastern Star* (The Cockpit Theatre), and *She Ventures and He Wins* (Rose Playhouse).

Earlier this year she formed part of Dangerous Space, an all-female company launched to address the lack of multi-dimensional opportunities for actresses.

SUZY WONG: FITTING IN AND FUCKING UP
by KATHRYN GOLDING

Production History

Suzy Wong: Fitting In and Fucking Up was first developed through Royal Court's Live Lunch programme and, since then, through Paines Plough's Come To Where I'm From project. It was first performed at Theatre503 on the 24th April 2017 as part of Foreign Goods Last Forever 2: Visions Of England with the following cast and creative team:

Cast

Kathryn Golding

Creative Team

Writer	Kathryn Golding
Director	Grace Joseph
Producer	Jingan Young

SUZY WONG is a third-culture kid. Looks younger than she is.

SUZY: Growing up was – I mean, it wasn't – I mean it was, and it wasn't...

Let me start again.

I grew up in a liberal little town in the suburbs of London. I say town; it's more like a sleepy little village. A village that declares itself: 'The Home of England Rugby'.

On big match days, there are 80,000 people swarming through our tiny streets, spilling out of the pubs and curry houses – the village comes to a standstill on match days – the excitement is palpable. The atmosphere is like electricity pulsing through the streets.

As I make my way to the station, I see a woman, two chubby children hang from her arm in England shirts, belly ripe with another. A man in chinos and loafers nuzzles her neck affectionately.

I know this woman. I know her. As a girl, I knew her. And I stare, trying to work out how. I'm gawping but it's bugging me. And then it hits me:

School!

As the woman and I clock each other, doing the awkward nod and smile thing, I wonder why it is that we've stayed. It's a pretty sweet place to live. Mostly liberal. Mostly wealthy, middle-class people. Mostly white people.

There were no Black kids at our school and only a handful of Asians. It was equal parts privilege and a pain in the butt.

School wasn't a happy time for me. If you're an Asian kid, or you have an Asian parent, Saturday's just another exciting fun-filled day. And by that I mean more school. Chinese School is kind of like Sunday school but instead of Sundays, you go on Saturdays. And instead of learning about God, you learn how to be a model Chinese citizen.

I was terrible. Deliberately so.

See, being a model Chinese citizen means learning Mandarin; helpful everyday phrases such as:

SUZY AS CONFUCIUS: 'Before you embark on a journey of revenge, dig two graves.'

'Life is simple, but we insist on making it complicated.'

'Silence is a true friend who never betrays.'

SUZY: This is why I hate Confucius. He says a lot passive bollocks about how we should just let shit happen to us and accept what we've been given. Like this girl. I recognise her from regular school.

There was a gang. They'd call me all sorts. Some of the names I didn't even know what they meant but, from the tone, I could tell they weren't nice.

Once though – once – she called me 'Paki'.

I remember it confusing me. I was confused. You'd be confused too, right? My kid brain knew my dad was Chinese and that Chinese aren't from Pakistan. They don't get called 'Pakis'. That's what you called the brown kids, not the yellow ones.

I was five. The same week Tiananmen Square happened. All I could think was that I wished that I could be as brave as Tank Man. To stand against the bad guys. To stand in the face of oppression, unflinching, with honour.

Or whatever it is that five-year-olds think.

I always wondered what happened to him. Afterwards. He just disappeared...

Needless to say, growing up, I spent a lot of time in my head and watched a lot of Sci-Fi. I loved it. I got to see people like me on telly. It was either Sci-Fi, or Disney's Mulan.

When I grew up, I wanted to be a scientist. I know, I know: typical Asian goals. But, in space, there are all of these crazy bad guys to fight so no one bats an eyelid if you roll with a gay Asian and a man with a vagina for a forehead.

Some days I just wanted to scream 'beam me up, Scotty!'

    Beat.

When the rugby crowds come to town, they get tanked up early. Pre-gaming on the train. Cheers and chants ring through the air. Sometimes it's a call and response. Sometimes jovial abuse. And if you look closely, you can see the future leaders of our country – the Bullingdon types – all gilets and chinos.

And their favourite thing to shout at me? 'Where are you from?' Growing up, I didn't want to be different. No one wants that. And that 'where are you from?' makes you different. It sets you apart.

I get it. You meet someone who's different, who looks interesting, and you want to know about them. But people go on this *(she indicates her face)* because it's the first thing they see.

SUZY AS BULLINGDON TYPE: 'No, but where are you *really* from?'

SUZY: It's as though they're trying to catch me out and I'll be like: 'Shit! You got me. I'm a Romulan.' They make it sound like they know something I don't. With their 'knee hows' and 'kon-knee-chi-was'. Has that ever worked as a chat-up line? I mean, who would say that to someone else? 'That's really hot: talk Asian to me.' No, my dad isn't Jackie Chan. I can't do kung fu.

I'm shit at maths. Dairy gives me the chronic shits. Is that the kind of stuff people want to know? I'm British!

Beat.

Maybe it'd be easier if I did have a vagina on my forehead…

And you know what? I'm jealous. I'm jealous of other minorities. They have guts. No one says shit about the Pakistanis in case they get all Jihadi Extremist on them and Black people'd be like, 'I will fucking end you!' No one stands up for themselves. We're an easy target. We're so fucking weak!

SUZY AS CONFUCIUS: 'Life is simple, but we insist on making it complicated.'

SUZY: One night, I got into a debate with a friend and his mate butted in:

SUZY AS THE POLITICIAN: 'Err well, you know. Aside from Hong Kong, we never really colonised your end of the world. Sorry about the Opium Wars and that but it wasn't like us palefaces co-opted your culture. We don't feel the same kind of guilt so we don't need to make things up to you. You know, people from the subcontinent, West Indies and Africa, we've got loads more to answer for so we have to make a special effort.'

SUZY: What. The. Fuck?

'Paleface' is a Native American reference and I wish someone would tell Hollywood this because they just love co-opting other people's culture. And, you don't have anything to feel guilty for about East Asians? Because that's what equality is about, isn't it? Feeling guilty.

You're here so I'm preaching to the converted but I get this all the time. My mum tells me not to worry about it. She has this saying:

SUZY AS CONFUCIAN MUM: 'You can't expect both ends of the sugar cane to be as sweet.'

SUZY: Fucking Confucius.

The thing is, I get so frustrated. We're not known for standing up for anything. And when we do, like Tank Man, we disappear. Never to be heard of again. Hardly Gandhi. Or Martin Luther King. Or Nelson Mandela, is it? Truth is, we don't have much in the way of heroes to look up to. Confucius is our lamented, yet impotent, genius, Mao's a meglomaniac nutcase and let's not get started on the lil Kims of North Korea...

Maybe that's why we need a saviour like Matt Damon. Maybe that's why we need Scarlett Johansson and Tilda Swinton. Maybe, we don't deserve to save ourselves.

> *Beat.*

So anyway, there was me, and my friend's mate with his Selective Colonial Guilt, who I didn't know, listening to our mutual friend gently purring away. He spoke with such confidence and power about how he wanted to become a politician, how he wanted to change lives...

At some point, I must have fallen asleep. I don't know when but, when I woke up, I couldn't see my friend. I couldn't see much at all.

Pink and blue spots danced across my eyes, a heavy weight pressed down on me. An arm pinned me by my throat. I could barely breathe. But I could feel him.

I can't remember how long it went on for. Or when he stopped. I just remember – it's like flashes, like bubbles bursting in my brain – this ghastly '70s wallpaper, flashes of chintz. And, vaguely, somewhere, pain.

I don't know if I blacked out because I couldn't breathe or because that's what brains do when faced with trauma: they black out to protect you so that you don't go into shock. But I remember the pungent, salty, sweet smell of his sweat lingering on my skin.

Even now, in the crushing, claustrophobic Rugby crowds, I can smell it.

I didn't raise charges. I couldn't bear it. I couldn't bear hearing how it was my fault – what I'd been wearing, or if I led him on – but mostly, I didn't want to have to repeat what had happened. Live it, again and again...

You know, people in power take for granted that there won't be a fight because, probably, there won't be...

As I approach the train station through the throng of Rugby fans, I see him. The Politician with Selective Colonial Guilt. I see him scoop up the pudgy child from the pregnant woman's arm.

He does a double take. I can see it in his eyes: something. Some form of recognition. He looks away sharply.

SUZY AS CONFUCIUS: 'Silence is a true friend who never betrays.'

SUZY: No, Confucius, our silence is our consent and we're not going to be quiet anymore.

Kathryn Golding is a recognised emerging writing talent with a unique voice working across screen and stage.

Graduate of the Royal Court's Unheard Voices Programme, she is currently supported by the Edinburgh International Television Festival, and is part of the Year 5 Write To Play programme with Graeae Theatre company. She is working on projects for both theatre and television.

Recent credits include: *Being Suzy Wong* (Royal Court), *Play 13* (Vault Festival), Come To Where I'm From project (Paines Plough, with Tamasha Theatre) and *Suzy Wong: Fitting In and Fucking Up* (Theatre503).

JAMAICA BOY
by STEPHEN HOO

Production History

Jamaica Boy was first performed at Theatre Royal Stratford East on the 21st June 2015 with the following cast and creative team:

Cast
Daniel York
John Omole
Marcus Griffiths
Natalia Hinds
Yvonne Gidden
Stephen Hoo

Creative Team
Writer	Stephen Hoo
Director	Rikki Beadle-Blair
Producer	Karen Fisher & Team Angelica
Stage Manager	Sarah Buik

Jamaica Boy was also performed at Soho Theatre Studio on the 3rd March 2016 with the following cast and creative team:

Cast
Paul Hyu
Alex Kiffin
Nathan Clough
Natalia Hinds
Leo Wan
Anni Domingo

Creative Team
Writer	Stephen Hoo
Director	Topher Campbell
Producer	Chris Corner/Kumiko Mendl
Stage Manager	Sophie Mason

Characters

OPHELIA – Late 60s, Black, Jamaican, round. Speaks with a Jamaican accent.

CHRISTIAN – 20s, half Chinese/White, surly. Speaks with an urban London accent.

MISHECK – 20s, Black, sporty, wiry. Speaks with an urban London accent.

PYRO – 20s, Black, skinny, handsome, dark, geeky. Speaks with a London accent.

SCENE 1

Present day. London, Croydon. A garden/allotment. A tonne of mess. A shed.

OPHELIA stands facing CHRISTIAN who wears a hoodie. CHRISTIAN has his hood up almost totally covering his face.

OPHELIA: Late!

CHRIS: It's ten!

OPHELIA: Five past.

CHRIS: *(Kisses teeth.)* Shut up.

OPHELIA: Watch your mouth.

CHRIS: You gonna report me for being five minutes late? Waste gash!

OPHELIA: Yes. And it needs clearing.

CHRIS: You what?

OPHELIA: The waste. I want you to clear the waste. You see it there?

CHRIS: ...

OPHELIA: *(Handing him some gardening gloves.)* Move all of that to over there, then I want you to take up di slabs, put them in di wheelbarrow, I'll let you know what next.

CHRIS: What if I need a slash?

OPHELIA: Knock pon di door. I'll accompany you.

CHRIS: Fink you can treat me like a dog like?

OPHELIA: *(Mocking.)* A dog would do it outside. Like a dog like.

CHRIS: You don't know me, man.

OPHELIA: I know that you are a latecomer, I know I am *not* a man. And I know what you are here fi do.

CHRIS: Look –

OPHELIA: And I know what my function is.

CHRIS: And I know that I'm not a dog. I know my rights and I know that now it's ten past ten so you are making me more late, innit.

OPHELIA gets an instant Kodak camera out and takes a picture of CHRISTIAN.

CHRIS: Da fuck d'you fink you're doing?

OPHELIA: Proof of arrival.

She waits for it to process then waves it to dry.

CHRIS: What? Look...woman... I don't –

OPHELIA: Miss Randles.

Beat.

CHRIS: You didn't arsk my name.

OPHELIA: You didn't introduce yourself. You bowl in like dis. No manners, no courtesy. Just insolence. Probably born from a life of indolence, indifference and bone idle inertia.

CHRIS: What?

OPHELIA: Wha' wha' wha'. What this, what that, Wotless! Char!

OPHELIA opens a file she is holding.

OPHELIA: Chiang Weng O'Riordan.

CHRIS: It's Christian!

OPHELIA gives him a look. Snorts.

CHRIS: My name's Christian.

OPHELIA: *(Giving side eye, still drying the photo.)*
Umhem is required to fulfil the terms of community
service for a period of exactly 12 weeks.

CHRIS: ...

OPHELIA: Said offender will work for a period of 20
hours a week.

CHRIS kisses his teeth.

OPHELIA: Unpaid. Said offender will arrive on time.

CHRIS: I was.

OPHELIA: Will be subject to daily progress reports.
Punctuality reports.

CHRIS: Fuck's sake!

OPHELIA: Civility reports.

CHRIS: I know all this.

OPHELIA: Other conditions include: no back chat,
improved manners, and have a shower in the
morning. *(Wafting the report.)* Oh lordy! You g'warn
stink up the di place bwoy.

CHRIS: *(Trying to grab the report unsuccessfully.)* You're
making it up.

OPHELIA: He will not steal –

CHRIS: I ain't not no teef!

OPHELIA: Triple negative! Improve his grammar –

CHRIS: Where do I start?

OPHELIA: *(Pointing to shed.)* He will fetch the rake.

CHRIS: Where?

OPHELIA: *(Still in report tone.)* Where ya tink?

CHRISTIAN makes for the shed.

He will pull up him trousers and he will cover his mouth when him cough.

CHRIS: *(Offstage.)* When *he* coughs.

Clatter can be heard.

CHRIS: *(Offstage.)* Why d'you let this place get so mashup for?

OPHELIA: My knees aren't what they used to be. And it serves the community, 'cause now miscreants like yourself have something fi do.

OPHELIA checks the polaroid. CHRIS comes back from the shed.

CHRIS: Does it say what I done?

OPHELIA is staring at the polaroid. Then looks up at CHRISTIAN. He's an image of the past.

Beat.

CHRIS: Yo! Eh yo? Miss Randles?

CHRIS pulls off his hood. OPHELIA looks at him.

OPHELIA: *(Going inside.)* Clear up the mess.

CHRIS: *(Bemused.)* What? Kiss ma teef!

SCENE 2

OPHELIA's garden/allotment.

MISHECK and CHRIS are chatting. CHRIS is making a brick enclosure.

MISHECK: These people fam. Dat call themselves 'diversity role models' yeah. Go into schools and talk about gays. Like it's a good fing like. I mean literally coming into the school and doing show 'n' tell 'n' shit.

CHRIS: ...

MISHECK: Like what are they gonna show and tell? How to be a batty man? How to fuck another man in the arse? DRY! It's narsty. Pure narstyness. What is the world coming to? Homo-geddon. Believe.

Beat.

Why can't people see that heteronormative binary social structures exist for a reason bruv? A good reason. It's nature. The order of things.

CHRIS isn't listening as usual.

So fam, yo blud, yo cuz, you a gardener now is it? Is this your lot? It's fucking dumb. What happened to inspiring youngsters in situations? Gardening isn't inspiring. It's meditative. NOT inspiring.

CHRIS: It's supposed to be a punishment fool. A service to the community?

Beat.

MISHECK: *(Referring to inside the house.)* What's she like then?

CHRIS: She's a fucking xenomorph blud.

They laugh. CHRIS does an impression of the Alien from the 'Alien' films.

MISHECK: *(Sotto, referring to inside.)* Anything good?

CHRIS: Not allowed inside. Locked and bolted innit. She got a clip board, monitoring me and shit. Twitching the curtains. She got this community ting down to a T, ya get me?

MISHECK: *(Loudly.)* You ain't no house chigga then! You white bitch!

CHRIS: Shut up man, she'll come. She's Black. She's a granny.

MISHECK: COCONUT!

CHRIS: Shut. Up!

MISHECK: Some proper out in the plantation chigga innit cuz. She gotta have something worth something. Grannies keep wads of cash in tea pots innit. My granny did anyway. Before she put it all into a high interest rate ISA with nationwide 1.02% ya know!

CHRIS: Patience is a virtue blud. I told you she's hardcore. I wouldn't be surprised if she got laser beams 'n' shit in there.

They laugh.

CHRIS: I wanna sweeten her up but she's proper stamping on my balls over everything I do. Give it time. We'll see what's what. Antiques innit.

MISHECK: You ain't never been able to sweeten up gyal blud. And you ain't never had balls.

CHRIS: Ain't never had balls?

MISHECK: What?

CHRIS: 'Ain't never had balls' means I had balls all along fool. NOT NEVER HAD BALLS?

MISHECK: Shut up talking balls man. It's gay.

CHRIS: ...

MISHECK: Look yeah. If you can sweeten up an old biddy you're on the right path to actually getting lucky wiv gyal, ya get me? You gotta start somewhere innit. Yo bruv, I'm gagging to bash some fanny. Even granny fanny.

CHRIS: Argh! What has the world come to? Sickness runs deep with you.

CHRIS goes to move some clutter out of the way. Starts working on a new patch.

Truth yeah, why you ain't doing *your* ting like? Won't you get penalised?

MISHECK: You serious? They got me washing a wall. Like a wall. Just a big, white, don't even know what's behind it...wall. Community officer kicked me a mop and bucket and asked me to clean it. I dusted bruv, nah mate. Fuck that shit. Then I bounce here and look at you. A vision of broken Britain. Pussy whipped. Out in the garden like a slave from back in the day.

CHRIS: Bitch said if I break the rules I get into more trouble –

MISHECK: Rules! Listen chigga. We got into trouble fool. *This* is trouble. It's done. I'm trouble! I say it with pride bruv. What more can we get into?

CHRIS: We're losers Mish! *(Sarcastically.)* Broken Britain. You say it wiv pride?

Beat.

MISHECK: Yeah! I say it wiv pride. I've made peace with it. No more cognitive dissonance ya feel me?

CHRIS: ...

MISHECK: You're looking lost again. Come 'n' go yeah. Little bird tells me the sensors broken in Boots. Lifting is a peace of piss. I wanna get my hands on that No7 serum dem gyals go nuts for. Ebay that shit! *(Sings.)* Money money money moneeeeeey Money!

CHRIS: Pause! Real talk yeah. I wanna do this and move up. I don't wanna teef shit. Don't wanna beef with people.

MISHECK: We are products of the construct fool. This is the path of least resistance. Listen, Black man walks into a shop and doesn't teef shit it doesn't matter.

CHRIS: What moist shit you pontificating on now –

MISHECK: We enter the shop we've as good as teefed shit anyway, even if we ain't. These people's synapses already played out what they *think* we gonna do in milliseconds. Even if I walk out the shop and not done noffink –

CHRIS: Double negative. You lean?

MISHECK: Listen! The fact that they've already played out what I was gonna do remains... Trace trauma bruv. We already teefed it, *in their heads*, even if we didn't teef it, which we could've been there to do, which we ain't, cause you're lame. Chris! Come!

CHRIS: Mish, you always on some... Dem security guards are Black!!!

MISHECK: *(Over it.)* Nigerians though! You don't get it... Again.

CHRIS: I get these things. Projections.

MISHECK: So fuck it innit.

CHRIS: Why are you talking about teefing shit Mish? We ain't here 'cause we jacked stuff. We're here 'cause –

MISHECK: Same principle applies to acts of violence chigga. They put all of that and all of us in the same box.

CHRIS: And I'm not Black.

MISHECK: But you wear a hoodie innit.

OPHELIA comes out.

OPHELIA: Is wha' you do?

MISHECK: He's making you a brick wall innit. What's with all the walls man.

OPHELIA: Who are you?

MISHECK: Can't I chat with a bruva?

OPHELIA: No! You cyan't. Rules of community service. G'warn.

MISHECK: Fuck you bi –

OPHELIA goes for MISHECK who bolts. CHRIS looks lost in the commotion.

OPHELIA: Idiot pickney. Trespassing too.

CHRIS: What the fuck are you doing?

OPHELIA: Clearing away the strays. You know di rules. Now, I need you to run some errands.

OPHELIA: *(Handing a list.)* Soy sauce, garlic, ginger, spring onions, chicken breast and –

CHRIS: Fink I'm your slave?

OPHELIA: I thought you could do –

CHRIS: Wanna make up for the past is it?

OPHELIA: And what do you know about the past?

CHRIS: This is community service...not some plantation ting.

OPHELIA: What nonsense you talk?

CHRIS: Taking out your Black anger on me.

OPHELIA: Oh no my youth! You can't gwarn like that –

CHRIS: I cleared your shit. I did what you said. I filled those bags with rubbish and you still up in my business like some Wendy Williams interview.

OPHELIA: Wendy what? Look. Chris.

CHRIS: You wanna treat me like a dog –

OPHELIA: Christian!

CHRIS: I could complain you know. I still got rights.

OPHELIA: Christian.

Beat.

OPHELIA: I thought I could cook for you tonight.

Beat.

CHRIS: Don't like Chinese.

OPHELIA: Try it.

CHRIS: It's bad for you. All the oestrogen. Soya. Makes you a batty man. It's gay.

OPHELIA: What trash you talk?

Beat.

OPHELIA: Your ingratitude is beneath contempt.

CHRIS: Fry cats and dogs innit.

OPHELIA: Please. You are talking some Fu Manchu complex right now.

CHRIS: Saves them money. Reuse the oil for years. Like you can cook Chinese food.

OPHELIA: You want it or not?

CHRIS: *(Puts hand out.)* Whatever. Cash.

OPHELIA slips him twenty pounds. CHRIS makes to go then turns.

CHRIS: What's Fu Manchu?

SCENE 3

OPHELIA's garden/allotment.

Traditional Chinese music blends into the sound of the inner city. CHRIS and OPHELIA in the garden.

OPHELIA: These are long lasting bulbs. Hyacinths, Tulips, Daffodils –

CHRIS: You want them over there then?

OPHELIA: They will look better here.

CHRIS: Sun shines over there though innit.

OPHELIA: I suppose you're right. Maintaining a continuously flowering garden is a strategic operation. We want sixty to eighty days of colour from these bulbs.

OPHELIA potters about.

CHRIS: Don't mess up that area please.

OPHELIA: *(Moving stuff.)* Developing manners too. I'm off to a community meeting now. So please don't break up my garden digging for China.

OPHELIA messes up a patch of the garden with her curiosity.

CHRIS: What did I just say?

OPHELIA: I think you may have found your calling Christian. What about that patch over there?

CHRIS: I'm gonna grow vegetables there. I've been reading up on it on Google.

OPHELIA: A cottage garden? I guess you want some money to buy the seeds?

CHRIS: Yeah.

OPHELIA: I'll get some money out when I go to see Doctor Ram tomorrow. You sure you don't want to do it over there?

CHRIS: Nah. Leave that area man.

OPHELIA: You want me to cook tonight?

CHRIS: No.

OPHELIA: Suit yourself.

OPHELIA goes to make her way back in with her bag and coat.

OPHELIA: You sure you don't want me to cook.

CHRIS: Chinese?

OPHELIA: Wasn't that bad was it?

CHRIS: A bit gooey. But okay.

Beat.

CHRIS: How about I cook?

OPHELIA: Oh no no no my youth!

CHRIS: I could do laz-ag-nee.

OPHELIA: You can't even pronounce it.

CHRIS: It was a joke. You think I'm stupid?

OPHELIA: I don't think you're stupid Christian. Look what you've done to the garden. Divided up the place nicely. Mathematical. Always good with the numbers you lot.

CHRIS: I'll do jerk chicken.

OPHELIA: Oh and how do you make jerk chicken?

CHRIS: Google.

OPHELIA: You're not messing up my kitchen bwoy.

CHRIS: Not allowed inside anyway.

OPHELIA: That too.

CHRIS gets out an old black and white photo of OPHELIA. She is standing next to a Chinese Jamaican man in his 20s, handsome and angular.

CHRIS: Who's this?

OPHELIA: Where you find that?

CHRIS: Shed.

Beat.

CHRIS: I was looking for spades and stuff.

OPHELIA: It was locked.

CHRIS: It was. He looks Chinesey like.

OPHELIA: He is 'Chinesey like'. Like you.

CHRIS: My mum was Irish.

OPHELIA: Your name is Chiang Weng –

CHRIS: It's Christian!

OPHELIA: But the force is strong in you bwoy.

CHRIS: You some Jamaican Yoda?

OPHELIA: You are Chinese.

CHRIS: Half.

OPHELIA: Yes. Half Chinese.

CHRIS is irritated.

OPHELIA: I know you are half Irish.

CHRIS: Yeah.

OPHELIA: Just like I know that you are half Chinese.

CHRIS: So?

OPHELIA: I know that you are petulant.

CHRIS: You said I developed manners –

OPHELIA: And I know that you are making me late for my meeting. *(The photo.)* Give me that! Stop snuffling about my things or you'll get another strike on your form.

CHRIS: Another? What was the first one?

OPHELIA: Bad hygiene!

CHRIS: That ain't fair. You can't give me strikes for no reason.

OPHELIA: Watch me.

Exit OPHELIA. We enter into a dreamscape flashback. The past. CHRIS is talking to PYRO.

CHRIS: Yeah. Half Chinese.

PYRO: Ni Hao Ma?

CHRIS: What's that?

PYRO: Ni Hao Ma? You should know. You're half Chinese.

CHRIS: I don't know. Happy New Year?

PYRO: No that's Xin Nian Kuai Le. But you gotta pay attention to the tones. It's tonal. There are four tones and a neutral tone.

CHRIS: How do you say 'I am Chinese'?

PYRO: Wo Shi Zhong Guo Ren. Say it.

CHRIS: *(Pronounces it incorrectly.)* War Shur Zong Gor Ren.

PYRO: Why do you keep looking round?

CHRIS: Mish and my boys will be coming soon innit.

PYRO: Oh. So, like just gotta 'keep it real like'.

CHRIS: Affirmative.

They laugh.

PYRO: Wanna go to Littleheath Woods later? Pretend we're in the holodeck. Or we could go Forbidden Planet? Gonna order the NCC-1701.

CHRIS: Come on man. We're too old for that shit.

Beat.

Anyway, NCC-1701 is gay man. You know it's all about the NCC-1701-D.

PYRO: Negative.

CHRIS: Positive.

PYRO: Okay, neutral.

CHRIS: Zone.

Beat.

CHRIS: *(Smiling.)* You're a dickhead.

MISHECK: How can an inanimate object have a sexual orientation?

We hear the arrival of MISHECK and friends.

CHRIS: I'll tell you later. You best dust.

SCENE 4

OPHELIA's garden/allotment.

CHRIS is with MISHECK.

MISHECK: Is it ready?

CHRIS: You ain't smokin' my weed bruv.

MISHECK: To sell you dickhead. We gotta sample it at least.

CHRIS: You're not wasting product. This is capital. It ain't ready.

MISHECK look confused. CHRIS ushers him over to the weed plant.

CHRIS: I gotta check if this is male or female. She needs to be alone to produce the buds. The male plant just confuses her like.

MISHECK: ...

CHRIS: You're looking lost Mish. If it's male I gotta take it away from the female or else it could turn it into a hermaphrodite.

MISHECK: What the fuck are you talking about. Hermaphra-what?

CHRIS: Not male, not female...sort of being both at the same time like.

MISHECK: This is some Caitlyn Jenner shit.

CHRIS: It ain't ready.

MISHECK: Where you learning all this man and woman and hermaphra-greek-ting from?

CHRIS: Google innit.

MISHECK: Nah nah nah, Miss 'Jamaica Jamaica' schooling you innit? She on some proper hydroponic ting?

They laugh.

CHRIS: She don't smoke. She just watches me through the nets.

MISHECK: You been inside yet?

MISHECK makes for the door.

CHRIS: Don't go inside.

MISHECK: Chill yeah. I won't touch nothing. Just wanna do a bit of recon.

CHRIS: Community service remember? You're jeopardising me.

MISHECK: Jeopardising? Dictionary boy now? She teaching you English Clit is it?

CHRIS: You're gonna get me in shit.

MISHECK: *(Incredulous.)* You fucking planted a weed plant in her garden!

MISHECK goes to the door. It's not locked.

MISHECK: See....didn't even break in.

MISHECK goes in. OPHELIA comes back carrying shopping.

OPHELIA: Chris can you help me with this?

CHRIS: Oh hey. Miss Randles check this out.

OPHELIA: What?

CHRIS: I planted chillies.

Distracting her away from the back door.

OPHELIA: Good. I need to put this in the kitchen.

She goes to walk in the house.

CHRIS: Miss Randles.

OPHELIA: Call me Ophelia.

CHRIS: The guy in the picture yeah, was he your friend? Or colleague?

OPHELIA: He was a –

CHRIS: What's his name like?

OPHELIA: His name was 'like' Chong. Well, actually it was Chong, no 'like' about it.

CHRIS: Was he the one who taught you how to cook gooey Chinese food?

OPHELIA: He couldn't even organise a cup of water.

CHRIS: So he spoke like Chinese is it?

OPHELIA: Occasionally yes but he was Jamaican.

CHRIS: So he spoke like you?

OPHELIA: Of course.

CHRIS: That's fucking funny man. I'd love to see that.

Beat.

OPHELIA: I think the way you speak is funny man...like.

MISHECK sneaks out as OPHELIA talks, oblivious, distracted.

You changed your tune. Seeking your roots all of a sudden. You have to know where you came from to know where you're going. I'm full of pearls of wisdom like that. *(Amusing herself.)* You should see my fridge magnets.

CHRIS: I'm from Croydon.

OPHELIA: Your family? Your heritage? Your background? Your blood?

CHRIS: Mum's Irish...was Irish, dad left.

OPHELIA: Did he ever speak Chinese to you?

CHRIS: *(Pondering.)* He tried. Then he left.

OPHELIA: And you never tried to contact –

OPHELIA smells a fish. Notices the patch where CHRIS is growing weed. MISHECK sneaks out but observes them from afar. CHRIS can see MISHECK escaping.

What dat?

CHRIS: What's what?

OPHELIA: You think I'm stupid? That looks like a ganja situation right there.

MISHECK enjoys watching CHRIS getting caught.

CHRIS: No, it's not! It's the Geraniums and shit!

OPHELIA: You're doing it all wrong.

Beat.

CHRIS: What?

OPHELIA: It needs sunlight. Proper sunlight light.
You need to cover it up with a plastic box.

CHRIS: And punch holes in it?

OPHELIA: Correct.

CHRIS: And you gotta use chopsticks, like a support.

OPHELIA: Yes.

Beat. OPHELIA goes to go inside. Stops. MISHECK looks on. Envious...

Your mother was Irish then?

CHRIS: I ain't chatting about that.

SCENE 5

OPHELIA's garden/allotment.

CHRIS is in the garden. PYRO is back.

CHRIS: Pyro! You can't just come back like this. There are rules. Now fuck off.

PYRO: I wanted to see you. Sort things out.

CHRIS: Pyro!

PYRO: I think it would be a good thing. To sort things out. I am gonna talk to Misheck too.

CHRIS: Are you fucking dizzy?

PYRO: For a few months I was, yes.

CHRIS: You know what I mean. You can't do this.

PYRO: Put you in a difficult position? What? Like face up to things?

CHRIS: ...

PYRO: What about me? The things I gotta face up to? The things I had to face? You should know about face, saving face, Chinese concept innit.

CHRIS: You don't get it.

PYRO: I do. You were saving face and I got my face mashed.

CHRIS: You're gonna get me in trouble.

PYRO: Already did.

CHRIS: Fuck off, fuck off, fuck off!

OPHELIA comes out.

OPHELIA: Why another ruckus inna my yard?

CHRIS: Tell him to go. He shouldn't be here. No friends allowed remember?

OPHELIA: Friends? This don't look too friendly to me.

CHRIS: Anyone.

OPHELIA ponders a moment.

OPHELIA: Talk.

CHRIS: What?   **PYRO:** Okay.

CHRIS: No.

OPHELIA: If you two don't talk it out. Chris you're getting a strike.

CHRIS: That ain't fair. You can't –

OPHELIA: Three strikes and you're community service order is extended and re-evaluated and you end up washing walls at the back of the Whitgift Centre.

CHRIS: You can't do that.

OPHELIA: You already got two Christian.

CHRIS: Why? For what?

OPHELIA: 'Cause I felt like it.

CHRIS: I'm surrounded by bitches.

OPHELIA: *(About to write on Chris's report.)* Uhmm...

CHRIS: Okay!

Awkward silence. No one wants to talk.

PYRO: *(Out of the blue.)* Basically Chris is a closet homosexual trapped in a straight, pussy-aspiring, grime, street, road man persona and he is extremely unhappy about it –

CHRIS: Oi!

PYRO: We were having an undercover bromance whilst I was teaching him Chinese and gently encouraging him to lift himself out of a ridiculous reality he'd created for himself.

CHRIS: It's not that simple –

PYRO: All the while we were both secretly bonding over the fact that both of our mothers died a year ago, mine from suicide and his from a drug overdose. As time went on it was pretty clear that Chris had a proclivity towards *Star Trek* whilst also liking the type of people who are born and labeled XY if you know what I'm chatting about...like.

Beat.

I just came to say hi really. It was nice meeting you again Miss?

OPHELIA: Randles

PYRO: Bye Chris.

PYRO leaves.

OPHELIA: He seemed nice.

CHRIS: You don't know what you're fucking with.

CHRIS goes to inside the shed and gets his stuff.

OPHELIA: Er, didn't I tell you not to go inside there?

CHRIS: Where else am I gonna keep my stuff?

CHRIS goes to leave.

OPHELIA: Er, it's not time yet. You're getting a strike.

CHRIS: Give me one then.

OPHELIA: Don't forget to pick up my prescription. Chris! Chris?

THE END.

Stephen Hoo studied Theatre at The Brit School before completing his BA in Modern & Classical Chinese at SOAS. He completed his MA in Theatre Lab at RADA. He was a member of the Royal Court's Critical Mass writing programme, and of BBC's Writers Room.

THE STONE
(or NO ONE DISASTER IS TOTAL)
by AMBER HSU

Production History

The Stone (or No One Disaster is Total) was first commissioned by the Royal Court Theatre and presented at the Jerwood Theatre Upstairs as part of Live Lunch Hidden — a group show interrogating the hidden narratives of British East Asian lives. It was performed on the 19th and 20th June 2015 with the following cast and creative team:

Cast

Vera Chok
Lourdes Faberes
Alice Hewkin
Andrew Koji
Andrew Leung
Daniel York Loh

Creative Team

Writer	Amber Hsu
Director/Producer	Lucy Morrison

Additional productions include performances at The Bunker Theatre and Theatre503 with the following cast and creative team:

The Bunker Theatre Bunker Without Borders Festival (5th April 2017)

Cast

Eugenia Low
Velda Hassan
Martin Sarreal
Siu Hun Li

Creative Team

Writer	Amber Hsu
Director	Mingyu Lin

Theatre503 - Foreign Goods Last Forever 2: Visions of England (24th and 25th April 2017)

Cast

Eugenia Low
Velda Hassan
Windson Liong
Yung Nguyen

Creative Team

Writer	Amber Hsu
Director	Mingyu Lin

Characters

GIRL

MOTHER

WANDERING WOMAN

MAN

OLD MAN

YOUNG MAN (of tragic, fragile quality)

A GRIM WOMAN NAMED LAURIE

This play is for at least three actors (but better with more). For a cast of three actors, the roles might be allocated as follows:

GIRL

MOTHER/WANDERING WOMAN/A GRIM WOMAN NAMED LAURIE

MAN/OLD MAN/YOUNG MAN

Setting

This piece is to be played with little or no set, or with minimally symbolic indications of setting which are:

A) a small home in a faraway village;

B) the top of a distant hill;

C) the interior of a lorry;

D) a modern brothel;

E) a river and its banks;

F) a town.

This play is for multiple actors. The lines are to be individually assigned to different characters/actors unless a character is specified, in which case, the line should be played as dialogue by the designated character. Where 'Pause' is written as dialogue, it is spoken. Each actor/character has a stone.

Note: Though this play is largely tragic, it can also be played with great humour – however sinister, sad, or grotesque.

— Somewhere elsewhere a thousand years ago, a man takes the rib of a boy and the shin of a girl and breaks all the bones in between.

— Pause.

— Somewhere elsewhere a hundred years ago, a woman takes the heel of her foot and the ball of her toes and breaks all the bones in between.

— Pause.

— Somewhere elsewhere, some years ago, a woman takes a girl from the crook of her gut into the cradle of her arms, and with that, a stone is born.

— Pause.

— One day the stone falls into the palm of her hand and turning it over and over the woman says to the girl:

MOTHER: — 'Gather before me my beloved. In the other room your father lays slain on the kitchen table. There is no longer hope for us here. The time has come for you to go. I give you this stone. Take it with you in the palm of your hand. With it goes all of my hopes and good intentions.'

MOTHER places a stone in the GIRL's hand.

— And in their imaginations, a shutter clicks. Lights flash. And they promise themselves that this will be the moment that will span across all time and hold them together once and forever all.

— — — — — — — — — — — — — — — — — — — —

— Question:

— What brand of bathroom, kitchen, or floor cleaner works best on blood stains?

— A shutter clicks.

— Lights flash.

— Pause.

— — — — — — — — — — — — — — — — — — — —

— In the morning a man arrives bearing a stick with the head of a snake on it. He turns to the girl and says:

MAN: — 'Where we are going is the place where your future awaits you. You will have food, shelter, and more work than you will know what to do with.'

— The girl follows him to the top of a hill where a lorry stands on its crest.

— The sunlight is white and sharp.

— It bounces off the steel corners of the truck.

— And staring at the sky that presses its weight against the mud in an endless horizon,

— The girl wonders if it will look just the same wherever it is they are going.

— — — — — — — — — — — — — — — — — — — —

Women, children, and an elderly man gather. They are all in rags.

— Inside the lorry, the girl finds herself squeezed into the darkness with:

— Twenty-eight women.

— Seven children.

— And one elderly man.

The OLD MAN coughs.

— He will not survive the journey.

The OLD MAN drops dead.

— At first the girl feels sorry for him.

A few GIRLS feel sorry for the OLD MAN.

— *All* the girls feel sorry for him.

All the GIRLS feel sorry for the OLD MAN.

— But this only lasts until the stink of his rotting skin becomes unbearable.

— At which point,

— Understandably,

— They start to hate him.

A commotion occurs in the lorry.

The MAN with Snakehead enters the lorry.

— —

— Question:

— What is the minimum length of rope necessary to immobilise the wildly flailing arms of 7 children and 28 uncooperative women?

— A shutter clicks.

— Lights flash.

— Pause.

— —

— After an unknowable amount of time, the girl finally emerges from the lorry into the light, where she is taken to a building on the edge of a strange town.

— And finds herself in the care of a fat, sweating woman named Laurie who says:

A GRIM WOMAN with a name tag that says LAURIE.

LAURIE: — 'Here you will have food, shelter, and more work than you will know what to do with. Your future awaits you.'

— The girl spies the letters on the fat, sweating woman's name tag.

— But the similarity between the name of her transportation mode and the figurehead of her incarceration is lost on her due to her rudimentary knowledge of English and the lack of a future time in which to learn otherwise.

— She awaits with anticipation her first day of work wondering if

— A) the restaurants here give away their leftovers,

— B) the house she will clean will have children or dogs, or

— C) the factories have indoor or outdoor toilets.

— She does not yet consider questions of men who stand in line waiting their turn to heave themselves onto the women and children one at a time until they burst.

A MAN enters.

— — — — — — — — — — — — — — — — — — — —

— Question:

— What is the equivalent force of a man weighing 14 stone and accelerating at a rate 1.4 times that of gravity against a still object?

— A shutter clicks.

— Lights flash.

— Pause.

— — — — — — — — — — — — — — — — — — — —

GIRL stands alone and isolated. Across from her stands a fearful YOUNG MAN, who is afraid to look at GIRL.

— After another unknowable amount of time, and countless uncles and fathers, the girl befriends a dull and dim-witted pig of a boy.

— Who has been sent there by an uncle who is determined to make a man of him yet.

— But he is only able to stand in the corner and stare.

YOUNG MAN finally looks at GIRL, shyly at first. Then YOUNG MAN looks away.

— Unable to bear the touch of another human being, he begs her not to tell a soul lest he be made a fool of.

YOUNG MAN and GIRL share a moment of tenderness and understanding.

— How strange she thinks, that in this land a man is as afraid of being a fool as a woman is of being beaten and raped.

— She promises him her silence.

— And in a moment of gratitude he promises to help her escape.

Pause.

_ _

— On the day of the planned escape she takes a stone from under the mattress, where it has steadily endured the felted and cottoned thrusts of thousands and thousands of bodies above.

— The moment it touches her skin she feels once again all the hopes and intentions of a faded and distant

> memory, rising up again to span across all time.

YOUNG MAN enters.

> — It holds her together with such an unknowable strength that she hardly feels a thing when the dimwitted pig of a boy enters the room and stands before her and says:

YOUNG MAN: — 'I will be a man yet.'

> — And proceeds to break all of her bones.

YOUNG MAN breaks the bones of GIRL.

> — Holding the strength of the stone in the palm of her hand,

> — She greets his blows as if she has been ready for it her entire life,

> — *(Softly.)* As if a spell was incanted somewhere, elsewhere,

> — Sometime ago,

> — Before she was even born.

The GIRL is broken. Lights dim.

> — A shutter clicks.

> — Lights flash.

> — Pause.

The YOUNG MAN gently touches GIRL tenderly and with regret.

GIRL is carried to a river bank.

— — — — — — — — — — — — — — — — — — — —

— Question:

— What brand of running shoe is best for running through the woods when carrying an excess body weight on the shoulders?

— A shutter clicks.

— Lights flash.

— Pause.

— — — — — — — — — — — — — — — — — — —

The GIRL drifts in dim light.

— After being thrown from the banks of a neighbouring river, the girl finds herself adrift in a sea of thought.

— She wonders at the strange constellation of human transactions and chance that have brought her to this strange, new place, half way across the world from where she began.

— Lying prostrate in the water, she notices her eyes are no longer in a position to see the horizon where the sky presses its weight on the mud of the earth.

— All she can see instead, is the wide, untethered night above.

— And inside of her, a million thoughts fill with the want of escape into the black stars above,

— But her tongue stays thick and dumb, like a large stone, sandwiched between her jaws.

— Against which her teeth,

— Can only clack away uselessly in the dark.

— She closes her eyes and thinks,

— What use is it anyways?

— What I would have to say to the stars in an already starry sky.

— — — — — — — — — — — — — — — — — — — —

— Question:

— Of the approximately 6,000 or so languages expected to die in the next 35 years, what percentage would be classed as:

— A) A gradual death

— B) A bottom-to-top death

— C) A top-to-bottom death

— D) A radical death,

— or

— E) Biological death?

— A shutter clicks.

— Lights flash.

— Pause.

— — — — — — — — — — — — — — — — — — — —

— When next she opens her eyes the girl finds herself beneath the face of a wandering woman,

— Who sees the girl drifting broken in the water, and drags her to the shore.

— Looking at the girl with grim, motherly eyes, she says:

WOMAN: — 'You, girl, could have beeen my daughter.'

— And she pulls out from under the girl's tongue,

— A stone.

— — — — — — — — — — — — — — — — — — — —

— A shutter clicks.

— Lights flash.

— Pause.

— — — — — — — — — — — — — — — — — — — —

Men, women, and children wearing nice hats gather around the WOMAN and stone, while the GIRL remains adrift.

— In the town beyond the banks of the river,

— Far away from the building still burning with its corridors of sweating men and naked children,

— The wandering woman takes the girl's stone,

— And with it, all the hopes and
intentions of every star that ever spanned
across all time,

— Or the length of the entire universe,

— (As if ever a thing could be known.)

— So that all the people would gather,
from near and far,

— To listen to what the stone had to say –

The stone is passed around and touched greedily...

— Passing it from one hand to another –

— Fingering each line –

— Each scratch –

— Each scar –

— Of its smooth and simultaneously
stony surface.

— Squeezing it deep into the pits of their
palms –

— Touching it to their thirsty, straining lips –

— Placing it under the weight of their own
hungry tongues –

Pause.

— So that they too can pretend to know
what it feels like –

— To speak nobly of hardship and pain.

— — — — — — — — — — — — — — — — — — — —

Growing softer.

       — A shutter clicks.

       — Lights flash.

       — Pause.

The GIRL stands alone.

       — Question:

Silence.

— — — — — — — — — — — — — — — — — — —

       — Until finally, somewhere, elsewhere, sometime ago,

       — The wandering woman takes the stone back to the river,

       — Hoping to find the girl again.

       — But the river is filled with a million currents that each end in a different puddle, lake, or sea.

       — And the girl is long gone

       — And no one can say for sure which direction she went.

       — The woman pauses, ready to throw the stone back into the water

       — Hoping it will find the girl again.

       — But she remains unsure, wondering if it will only drift out to sea,

       — Where it will be worn down into a thousand grains of sand by the waves,

— Or if it will drift back to shore,

— And simply sink,

— Back into the mud.

— *(Softly.)* A shutter clicks.

— She pauses.

— *(Softly.)* Lights flash.

— She thinks –

— *(Softly.)* Pause.

Pause.

— That she should do something to make sure.

Pause.

— But then she looks up and down the river banks,

— Where she sees a million more stones like the one in her palm,

— *(Softly.)* A shutter clicks.

— Each one taken from the mouth of another.

— *(Softly.)* Lights flash.

— Into the length of the universe, across all time.

— *(Softly.)* Pause.

Pause.

— And she shrugs,

— Throwing the stone out into the distant water.

— Either way, she wonders,

— Will the outcome be just the same...

The WOMAN throws the stone to the body of the GIRL and exits.

The rest of characters each take their stones and do the same, exiting afterwards.

THE END.

Amber Hsu (徐碧莉//xúbìlì) is a Chinese-born, US-raised, UK-based writer and visual artist.

A graduate of the Royal Court's Studio Groups, and BBC's Writers Room, her work has been commissioned by and performed at various theatres including the Royal Shakespeare Company, Royal Court Theatre, Islington Youth Theatre, Orange Tree Theatre and National Theatre.

In 2014, her first short film, *Next Time*, received a London Calling Award and was commissioned by Film London. In 2016, her short film script *The Match Girl* was produced by BBC Three for their groundbreaking series #TheBreak.

She is currently under commission with the Royal Shakespeare Company to develop stage adaptations of Chinese classics, and was named on the BBC's New Talent Hotlist in 2017.

She is also the creator of an artzine called *Tiny Pencil*, and the inventor of One Pound Poems – a live poetry project.

Once, she also worked in a morgue.

www.amberhsu.com // @amberhsu

UNDER A BLOOD RED MOON
A play in one act
by LUCY CHAU LAI-TUEN

Production History

Under a Blood Red Moon started out as a short play commission from the Royal Court and was presented as part of Live Lunch Hidden under the title *Restrain Your Grief and Adapt to the Mishap*. It was performed in the Jerwood Theatre upstairs (script in hand) on the 19th and 20th June 2015 with the following cast and creative team:

Cast

Lourdes Faberes
Daniel York

Creative Team

Writer	Lucy Chau Lai-Tuen
Director/Producer	Lucy Morrison

Many thanks to the many British East Asian Artists who have helped me. Special thanks to Lourdes Faberes, Daniel York and The Royal Court

This play is dedicated to the memory of Junix Inocian, actor and friend

Characters

MA, CHU
MA, LI

CUSTOMER
GANG MEMBER

(JIAN) JACKIE CHAN
MR. CHAN
MRS. CHAN

MONA HING
IDA BRAMBLE

Suggested doubling

MA, CHU/MR. CHAN
MA, LI/MRS. CHAN
JACKIE/CUSTOMER/GANG MEMBER

CHU's take away It's a Wonderful Wok and a hospital morgue.

CHU's dead body is wheeled into the morgue covered by a white sheet. LI, CHU's wife enters and sits next to her dead husband.

CHU slowly sits up, the sheet falls into his lap. Newly dead CHU can still interact with those he knew and loved.

IT'S A WONDERFUL WOK

LI: They stamped on you like a bug. Twenty-three of them and they're out on bail. Unbelievable!
Police tried to charge me with aggravated assault!
I laughed.

CHU: Now I'm a one-eighty by one-fifty rectangle of news.

LI: 'Local news. Owner of It's A Wonderful Wok Chinese takeaway killed in an incident'.
It's all over the TV. They rushed you to A&E, but you died before they could get you there.
I'm so mad at you!
For leaving the shop – for leaving me –
You were always telling me...

CHU: Stay inside, don't get involved...

LI: It's none of our business.

CHU: I thought you'd be happy, I did what you asked.

LI: He's back –

CHU: And he's not alone...

LI: So many of them!

CHU: Why are they screaming?

LI: Get away from the window.

CHU: Call the police!

LI: You call the fucking police!

CHU: Look!

LI: What?

CHU: The moon...

LI: Eh?

CHU: It's important...

LI: Not a good time...

CHU: 'When the moon is shining...'*

LI: Make this stop! Or – I'm done!

GANG MEMBER: Fucking Chinky-Changalings!
What right do you have to come over here?
Walk down our streets? Live in our neighbourhoods?

LI: Chu! Come back! Chu!

CHU: Who would have thought, my last memory, feet.
I was a man so I swallowed the insults.
I don't make a fuss, I don't draw attention to myself.
I knuckle down, I pay my taxes.
I work, work, work.
'I had no fear of the long road.'

CHU drops to his knees.

A boot cracks the back of my skull, then stops.
I thought, oh, it's raining. Then the smell. They were
pissing on me I look up and I focus on the blood red
moon.

BLACKOUT.

---

*the cripple becomes happy for a walk.

HOSPITAL MORGUE

LI: That Chinese lawyer turned up. The one you don't like. If it hadn't been for him, I'd be in prison.

CHU: See what happens when we draw attention to ourselves?
'Life is ruled by letting things take their course. You don't rule it by interfering.'

LI: I didn't ask for attention! Just help, because you failed.

CHU: Li, 'is not whether I failed, but whether you were content with my failure.'

LI: I'm here, only, I don't know where 'here' is anymore. This is where all our sweat, long hours and your platitudes have gotten us?
Now would be a good time for one of your stupid sayings!

CHU: 'Laws control the lesser man; right conduct controls the greater one.'

LI: Stubborn old goat!
Why didn't you talk to the police when I asked you to?

CHU: I talked to them.
Told them all about the trouble, the kids with bottles, swearing, pissing and shitting.
They laughed, accused me of wasting police time.
Putting on an accent. Accent? I don't have an accent.
'Teenage high spirits, a bit of harmless fun. Have you got proof? Not a lot I can do for you without proof, Sir.'
I knew you'd be upset. Better for you to be angry with me. So I said nothing.

LI: Every time I call the police, I have to tell them, my name is not Chu, it's Mrs. Ma!
Walking to the hospital, all eyes staring at me.
Whispering,
'That's the wife of the dead chinky. What's she doing out on her own?'

Huh! We Chinese only come in multi-packs, chopsticks
and bowls included. Before I entered the hospital,
I glanced up. There it was, your bloody red moon.

CHU: I told you...

LI: I... I would never have left you.

CHU: 'We earned a living by what we did, we made a life
by what we gave.'

LI: We were first to our business and the last to our beds.

CHU: It's, 'the first to the field and the last to the couch.'

LI: We had no time for anything but business.

CHU: 'Married couples who love each other tell each
other a thousand things without talking.'

Silence.

I now wish for so many things.
To have held you more often.

IT'S A WONDERFUL WOK

LI: What would you like?

CUSTOMER: 22, 45 and a (*leering at LI*) number SIXTY-NINE!

An awkward beat. LI looks at the CUSTOMER.

CUSTOMER: Whatchu staring at chinky bitch?
Cat got your tongue? Nice pusssy, pusssssy...

CUSTOMER suggestively waggles his tongue.

Wot, you no, spleakie Engrish?

LI: Yeah, I SPEAK ENGLISH.

CUSTOMER: Tsk, tsk! This – all mine – right down (*looks at LI*)
to the kitchen sink!
I'll be back Chinky-Chus.

CUSTOMER exits.

HOSPITAL MORGUE

LI: Every time the police didn't come, I felt we were being punished for being Chinese.

IT'S A WONDERFUL WOK

CUSTOMER: Tsk! Tsk! This – all mine – right down (*looking at LI*) to the kitchen sink!
I'll be back Chinky-Chus.

CHU: Tofu eater!

LI: I suppose I should go and get the mop then.

HOSPITAL MORGUE

LI: Your head went down, you stopped looking at me, talking to me. The only thing that came out of your mouth, those stupid sayings!

CHU: Which you always got wrong.

LI: Why didn't you just turn to me and say,
Li, wife, my love...

CHU: It was my responsibility...

LI: Why didn't you say, 'I'm worried.'
I'd have worried with you. I'd have put up with you saying something about 'sad birds building nests in my hair.'

CHU: I would have said, 'adversity leads to prosperity.'

LI: You're dead. And I'm walking home alone, under your bloody red moon.
What is it with East Asians and the moon?
Moon festival, Mooncakes, Moon rabbits?
I knew it was bad.
I'm as guilty as you. Just another frightened, acquiescent Chinese, who can't even bury her husband properly.

Beat.

Which one of your stupid sayings can help me now?

CHU: 'Life is a walking dream, death is going home'?

LI: Death is not fucking walking home!
Death is demolition!

CHU: You had to spoil it.

Sigh.

LI: Grief is a draw you open, take a look, then slam it shut.

CHU: 'This is one day and it will not last forever.'

LI: Some help here, Chu?
You were so much better at this stuff than me.
Think Li!

She taps her head furiously.

I know I have to do – something...

CHU: You can't let me go hungry – over there...

LI: You eat over there!

CHU: Oranges are best...

LI: Oranges!

LI rummages through her bag.

Oranges!
I've got an extra strong mint, a half-eaten Twix,
a Werther's Original, Fisherman's Friend, two Opal
Fruits, a Kinder Egg – I wondered where that went to
– and a boiled sweet covered in fluff?

CHU: Then you burn money...

LI: I've only got a fiver...

CHU: God Li! Not real money, ghost money, pretend
paper money...

LI: But I've only got real paper money...

CHU: You get it from the temple...

LI: We're in a fucking morgue...

CHU: I saw a copy of the Metro in here...you can use the paper, to make paper money.
Place the food down for me to eat...

Pause.

LI: Why aren't you eating?

CHU: I don't really eat, it's symbolic, I'm dead...

LI: Oh...

CHU: Now you burn the paper money, NOT the real money it's...

LI: Symbolic –
Is an extra strong mint, half a Twix, a Werther's Original and fury boiled sweet enough?

CHU: Just have to hope no one's watching.

LI: It doesn't feel right.
I have to burn the real money.

Pause.

I'm doing this, are you ready?

CHU nods his head, gets back onto the trolley and covers himself with the sheet.

LI: I hope that they handle you with gentle hands.

LI holds up the five pound note and a cheap plastic lighter.

BLACKOUT.

IT'S A WONDERFUL WOK

LI sits in the semi-dark, apron on, spatula in one hand and cleaning rag in the other. She is in shock. The door opens and JIAN/JACKIE CHAN stumbles into the empty takeaway. He has been badly beaten up.

LI: Oh my god!

She rushes to help – places him in a nearby chair. Closes and locks the door pulling down the blinds and then turns on the lights.

JACKIE: Thank you.

Pause.

Is it that bad?

LI: Don't move – don't do anything, I'll go and get the first aid kit.

LI exits out back, she can be heard rummaging through draws and cursing.

JACKIE: Thank you –

LI re-enters arms full of bandages, TCP, scissors, gauze.

LI: I told you not do anything!

Beat.

LI goes about her business and starts to clean JACKIE's face up. It becomes very clear that JACKIE's injuries are serious and need hospital care.

JACKIE: I'm sorry.

Beat.

About your husband.

Beat.

It shouldn't have happened.

Beat.

I just wanted to –

LI: Thank you –
You have to go to the hospital – this is beyond me –

JACKIE: Can't you just patch me up?
I'll be fine –
I just need to rest a little, I just /

LI: You need a proper doctor – if you won't go to the hospital
then let me call someone for you. Your mother or father /

JACKIE: No!
Please leave my parents out of this.
I'll let you put me in a cab and I'll go to the hospital
I promise.
My parents don't need to be bothered by this /

LI: What is it with you men!
You'd rather die than ask for help?

JACKIE: It's nothing like that –

LI: Was it them?
That beat you up? The same ones that, that –

JACKIE: Probably –
I don't know.
I don't want to upset you Mrs. Ma.

LI smiles.

What did I say that's so funny?

LI: You called me by my name, Mrs. Ma.
Do you know not one person got it right tonight –
they couldn't even get my husband's name right.

Beat.

So, what's your story?

JACKIE: I don't have a story.

LI: Chu said everyone has a tale to tell – whether it's a
tale worth hearing – that's another matter entirely.

JACKIE: It's the usual tale then –
I'm not the son that my parents want.
I can't be the son that my parents need.
I'm –

LI: Wouldn't have anything to do with the good looking young man you meet up with who always orders fried dumplings, egg fried rice, chili straw beef with bak choi and Chinese mushrooms in soy sauce?

JACKIE: How did you –
Are you a witch or /

LI: Just a woman's intuition.

Beat.

You need to get to the hospital. I'll call a cab it'll be quicker.

LI goes out back, you can hear her using a landline.

JACKIE: I'm sorry I didn't mean to – after all that you've –
Well you know –

LI: Chu's gone.
I'm just doing what Chu would have done.
Come on let me finish cleaning you up and then we'll get going.

JACKIE: My parents expect me to be the dutiful son,
to work in the shop when I'm not studying, to get married, to have children. If you're someone like me then that's never going to happen – not naturally.

LI: Loving in silence is worse than not being loved.
Not telling someone that you love them – you think there is time enough for everything – but you're wrong.
Come on let's get you to the hospital.

LI helps JACKIE up onto his feet, there is the sound of a car horn. LI and JACKIE walk slowly towards the door.

BLACKOUT.

HOSPITAL ICU

JIAN/JACKIE lies in a single side ward in the ICU, both arms and one leg is in plaster, he stares at the blood red moon.

JACKIE: It was only a matter of time –
Left me!
Fucking left me –
'A strategic withdrawal.'
Fuck you!

I look at the old Chinese couple who run the local takeway – they've been there as long as I can remember.
I watched them work day in day out – I don't want that to be my life –
Why can't I just be?
It was the wrong place, the wrong time –

His eyes staring up at the moon almost smiling and then whatever internal spark the old man had, withered –

I just covered my head and prayed.
I counted the grains of gravel as they bounced up and down.
What I wanted was to crawl away – to leave – to put as much space between me and that pathetic old man –

Police came and questioned did I 'know anything' about 'the vicious attack' outside 'The Wonderful Wok'.
I pretended not to understand what they were saying and dropped off to sleep.

Who thinks up these ridiculous names?
Fu King Chinese,
Tang Tastic,
Fook Yue,
Lo Fat,
Hard Wok Café and
What the Fok?

Beat.

Does it not occur to them that they're inviting people
to take the piss?
As if we need to make it easier!
I come home a week later, there in bright yellow
flashing neon, Hokkei The New.
We're nowhere near Scotland, we're not even north of
Watford!
The name before that was some distant relative,
Wang King.
I told him but he just wouldn't listen. He said I didn't
know what I was talking about, didn't understand
Chinese business.
When the recent trend for Pho came in, Dad wanted
to change the name to Mo'Pho Chinese.
He knows nothing about Pho, nothing about Korean
cuisine.
Next batch of name changes, equally cringe worthy:
Ho Le Chit,
Hu's up First,
Hoo Lee Chow,
Pho tastic – again with the fecking Pho,
Wok 'n' Roll.

Pause.

The only time Mum turned on Dad.
It freaked me out. I'd never seen Mum raise her voice.
It was a fantastic mixture of angry Chinese and
strangely formal English.

BLACKOUT.

THE CHAN'S HOME

MRS. CHAN: You stupid old man!
Spending so much time pouring over meaningless stuff,
pushing out more grey hairs over a restaurant name.
Who gives a shit what we name the restaurant!
All that matters is the quality of the food.

MR. CHAN: I'm just trying to make things better for us
woman!
You wouldn't understand /

MRS. CHAN: Don't I always do what you ask Ping? I'm the
good, dutiful wife.
And god knows why, I still love you.
I put up with all your ridiculous schemes.
When are you going to stop holding rice in your
stomach?
Cursing once a day is supposed to improve happiness
and lengthen life.
These days Ping, I'm cursing five, six times a day.
We don't do Pho, we're not Korean. Unless you're
going to hire a new chef, they don't come cheap.

Pause. MR. CHAN shakes his head.

As I thought. We're a small Chinese restaurant.
Serving honest, home-made food in generous
portions for a fair price.
Concentrate on that. Stop being foolish, pay more
attention to your son /

JACKIE: I'd never heard Mum talk like that before or
since.

Beat.

Mum and Dad don't know that I'm –
I can't talk to my parents about –
Mum has a mouth like a knife, but a heart like tofu.
She'd eventually come around, but Dad resolutely
traditional and inflexible.

MR. CHAN: How many times?
I've warned you to stay away from bad influences.
Stop trying to chase new trends.
Stay away from homosexual-related things.
The best way to do that is to get married!

JACKIE: *(Beat.)* I'm never going to be able to tell them.
I'm never going to be able to be myself as long as I
live at home.
I'll end up like the Chu Ma. Over worked, set upon and
dead.

*MR and MRS. CHAN enter. As soon as MRS. CHAN sees
JACKIE she starts to cry.*

JACKIE: Oh – Mum, please don't /

MRS. CHAN: What is it I must not do?

MR. CHAN: Calm yourself –

To JACKIE.

Don't speak to your mother like that, show some respect.

Beat.

Son, who did these terrible things to you /

JACKIE: I don't know Dad /

MR. CHAN: Don't know or won't tell?

MRS. CHAN: Are they treating you well?

JACKIE: Mum, this is a hospital not a prison!

MRS. CHAN: Don't get angry with me /

JACKIE: I didn't mean –
I'm just saying – you don't need to be afraid.

MR. CHAN: Says my son in a hospital bed with broken limbs!

JACKIE: Dad, that's not what I meant –

Silence.

MR. CHAN: How long?
Will you have to change when you go to university?

MRS. CHAN: Ping – leave him – look at him he's suffering /

MR. CHAN: Rong, this does not concern you /

MRS. CHAN: Does not concern me!
How can you say that to me?

Pause.

Have I ever interfered with your business?
Haven't I always been a good wife?

MR. CHAN nods.

This is my son.
Don't you dare tell me this does not concern me.
I am his mother /

MR. CHAN: You're making a scene.
Compose yourself.
Son, it is a blessing that you're here – we can talk.
You're always about to leave, just coming or just going out.
You're a man now, you're going to university, you'll make something of yourself.
We are not as young as we used to be. Which is why you need to plan for your future.
Our future.

MRS. CHAN: What your father is trying to ask is, how much serious thought have you given to your future, to your marriage, your wife and children?

MR. CHAN: How are you going to juggle your studies with work and the family business?

JACKIE: Dad!
If I go to uni it'll be in Leeds, Manchester – anywhere away from here!

JACKIE lets this news sink in.

I won't be living at home.
I won't be there to help with the family business /

MR. CHAN: There are good local universities /

MRS. CHAN: Stay at home, you won't have the expense of finding a flat /

JACKIE: If and I say IF I go to uni, it's not going to be in this area.
If I don't go to uni, I'm going to go travelling, see the world /

MR. CHAN: You can't do that.
Either you go to university and study or you come and work full-time in the family business /

JACKIE: You can't stop me, old man /

MR. CHAN: As long as you live under my roof you will do as I say /

MRS. CHAN: Ping – stop it /

MR. CHAN: I won't say it again Rong /

MRS. CHAN: Don't fight – look at him, he's not well.

She starts to tear up.

JACKIE: Mum please don't cry.

MR. CHAN: This is all your fault, upsetting your Mother!

Tries to soothe her, but she is not interested.

JACKIE: *(Takes in a deep breath.)* Since you're both here I –
There's something –
I have something –
It's about me – you need to know –

MR. CHAN: How are you ever going to get on in life if you can't say what needs to be said?

JACKIE: I'm, I'm, I –

Beat.

What's the point –
I'll never get married, I'm not the marrying type /

MRS. CHAN: Stop it –

Pause.

I understand /

MR. CHAN: Well I don't.

JACKIE: *(To the audience.)* She has a heart as soft as tofu.

MR. CHAN: What do you 'understand'?

MRS. CHAN: If you'd lift your eyes off the accounts once
in a while, you might not be so blind!

JACKIE: What do you understand?

MRS. CHAN: I'm your mother, I understand.

Pause.

You want me to say it out loud?

JACKIE: *(Cautiously.)* Say what out loud?

Looking at his dad.

MRS. CHAN: Our son is – different.

Silence.

MR. CHAN: I don't want different /

MRS. CHAN: Ping!
He is your flesh and blood, your son /

MR. CHAN: Either I have a son or I do not. There is no in
between!

MRS. CHAN: Ping!

MR. CHAN: Enough woman, time to go home /

MRS. CHAN: Jian, I will be back to see you later I /

MR. CHAN: *(Grabbing MRS. CHAN by the arm.)* Time to leave!

JACKIE: Let her go!

MR. CHAN: You will be too busy to come back /

MRS. CHAN: You may be too busy to come, but I will always make time to be with my son.

MR. CHAN: Do as you please!

Roughly releases his grip on MRS. CHAN.

JACKIE: Don't you ever grab Mum like that again or I'll /

MR. CHAN: Hitting is affection and scolding is love, all Chinese people know this.
If you want a lift home you come now. Otherwise take the bus or walk, I don't care.

MRS. CHAN: Leave me some money, I'll get the bus home.

MR. CHAN: I have no money, you'll have to walk home /

JACKIE: Mum – Dad –
Mum, I've got money, I'll get you a cab home.
Dad?

MR. CHAN: I'm leaving are you coming?

MRS. CHAN: You'll have to shut up shop without me Rong.

MR. CHAN: *(Beat.)* Tell Jian that I'll leave him his final weeks wages at the restaurant.

MRS. CHAN: You can tell him yourself, he's right here in front of you /

MR. CHAN turns his back and leaves.

MRS. CHAN: Give him time /

JACKIE: Sure.

MRS. CHAN: Don't you be disrespecting your father!
He'll come around.

JACKIE: When hell freezes over!

Beat.

Why didn't you say anything?

MRS. CHAN: It's not my place.
    You always had more light about you –

JACKIE: Yeah?

MRS. CHAN: Jian, unlike you our generation, those of
    us not born here, we still feel, stateless. Unrooted,
    unsettled in our souls.

JACKIE: Is that why Dad keeps changing the name of the
    restaurant?

MRS. CHAN: Perhaps.

Beat.

Your dad feels it more than he lets on.
    Not that we are not happy being here, having the life
    that we do –

JACKIE: Could have fooled me.

Pause.

Was it your idea to name me Jackie?

MRS. CHAN: What's wrong with being called Jackie?

JACKIE: Really, Mum?

Pause.

Seriously? Jackie Chan?

MRS. CHAN: Your dad, I was always a Bruce Lee fan.

*They both laugh – this sends JACKIE into a painful
coughing fit.*

JACKIE: I never knew you were into martial arts.

MRS. CHAN: There are lots of things that sons don't know
    about their mothers /

JACKIE: *(Pause.)* I can't believe that you knew and never let on once /

MRS. CHAN: The animals who did this to you, do you know them?

JACKIE: I don't know them and they don't know me.
I'm Chinese, I'm –
I speak perfect English, I know how to use a knife and fork.
People don't know what to make of someone like me.
I don't conform to their tick boxes. I'm not the uneducated, linguistically-challenged, heavily-accented Chink they expect me to be.

MRS. CHAN: Jian watch your mouth!

JACKIE: I'm just saying – that's how things are.

MRS. CHAN: Stop moaning, get out there and make friends /

JACKIE: So Dad can be rude to them?
That's why I stopped bringing school mates home.
He spat at one of my few friends because he was Black!

MRS. CHAN wrinkles her nose and shifts uncomfortably.

I thought if he can do that to someone he doesn't know, what is he going to do to his own flesh and blood when he finds out that I'm never going to be the son he wants me to be?

MRS. CHAN: Jian /

JACKIE: My wallet is in my jeans, there should be about thirty quid, take it, get a cab home and ring me.

JACKIE starts to cough, the coughing fit does not stop but gets worse, he starts coughing up blood, nurses and doctors rush in and MRS. CHAN is bundled out of the room. She is left waiting, watching as the curtains are pulled around her son's bed.

BLACKOUT.

114

PUBLIC PARK WAR MEMORIAL

MONA HING, a British East Asian pensioner.
IDA BRAMBLE, an English pensioner.

Early evening. IDA is sat on a park bench staring intently at a well-kept war memorial. She is well-dressed but her clothes have seen better days. MONA approaches carrying a large bag of shopping, she is dressed in a casual modern manner.

MONA HING: I got to ask lady. I see you every Tuesday and Thursday, sat on this bench. Doing – I don't know what you doing. Whatever it is, you doing it silently. With a face like the backside of an incontinent water buffalo.

IDA BRAMBLE: What I choose to do is my business.

MONA HING: No complaints on that one.

IDA BRAMBLE: If you don't mind...

MONA HING: No, I don't mind at all.

She sits down on the bench with a flourish. IDA does not acknowledge her.

What I do mind, well it's not mind so much as puzzle.
Why do you sit here every Tuesday and Thursday?
You meditating?
I'm no good at that, my mind it's too full of – stuff, memories –
Like a butterfly flitting from one thought to another.
My mind cannot settle these days.

IDA BRAMBLE: You're not going to stop talking are you.

MONA HING: You know me already! You're a smart classy lady.

IDA BRAMBLE: *(Sighs.)* What makes you say that?

MONA HING: Mona knows, I can tell from the cut, the material.
Best quality, the stitching –
It'll last longer than its owner.

IDA BRAMBLE: Were you a seamstress?

MONA HING: Me, no!
  I used to watch my aunts and uncles.
  Mona's hands, all thumbs /

IDA BRAMBLE: You mean you were all fingers and thumbs?

  MONA thinks and looks suspiciously at IDA. IDA looks at
  MONA properly for the first time.

  I've seen you too, watching me.
  At first, I thought you were just one of the bag ladies
  in the park. No offence meant /

MONA HING: None taken.

  Beat.

  What's a 'bag lady'?

IDA BRAMBLE: The women who stuff their lives in
  shopping trollies and endless carrier bags. So they
  can take it with them wherever they go /

MONA HING: What they do that for?
  Life is not some disembodied 'thing'.

IDA BRAMBLE: You don't get out much, do you?

MONA HING: I'm out all the time.
  Just not too many people see me.
  When they do they shout nasty things at me.
  Youngsters, no discipline these days.
  They flick unwanted food at me. What a waste!
  Or call me Ching Ching.
  When I first came here, I'm thinking Britain must
  be great place for the Chinese. You can become so
  famous everybody knows your name, even if they get
  the name wrong.
  Ching Chong must be really famous.

  Pause.

IDA BRAMBLE: That's not very nice.

MONA HING: Most people these days are not very nice.
Life is not very nice.

IDA BRAMBLE: I thought we were supposed to be living
in enlightened times. Diversity and multiculturalism...

MONA HING: World is all mixed up.
There is no balance. Summers here are still hit and miss.
I love the snow, it's beautiful, but only if I'm indoors.

IDA BRAMBLE: There are laws now that stop people from
being nasty or offensive.

MONA HING: Lady you're too much.
Laws, laws just scritchy-scratchy nonsense on paper.
Doesn't mean a thing if people don't put their heart in it.
Might stop them from saying things, but wont stop
them from thinking those things.
On the outside they're all nice.
On the inside they're rotten and ugly.

IDA BRAMBLE: You're very cynical.

MONA HING: Huh!
It's just the layers. I feel the cold.
It makes me look fatter than I am.
Never been called cylindrical before though!
Bit rude to call someone you don't know fat.

IDA BRAMBLE: That's not what I said, I said that you're
very cy-ni-cal.
Oh dear – how do I –
You're a very suspicious person – cynical.

MONA HING: *(Sniffs.)* You'd be cy-ni-cal if you'd lived my life.

Silence.

IDA BRAMBLE: I'm just angry all the time.
Even my own children tell me that I'm angry.

I sometimes think that life would be so much easier
if I was one of those people who'd settle for a walk in
the park to feed the pigeons /

MONA HING: Waste of time feeding pigeons, unless
you're going to kill and then cook 'em.

IDA BRAMBLE: *(Shocked.)* I really don't think you should
be doing that sort of thing – aside from the illegality /

MONA HING: Don't recommend it. Nasty, tough, very little
meat on them. I even tried my special chili, lime and
ginger marinade /

IDA BRAMBLE: Think of the health risks!

MONA HING: Only tried once, never again.
You were saying you are angry, why?

IDA BRAMBLE: Because –
You know I'm really not comfortable talking about /

MONA HING: You suffer from piles?
I've got cushion you can use?

*MONA pulls out a rubber ring cushion and starts to
inflate it.*

IDA BRAMBLE: It's very kind of you, I don't need it, I do
not have piles!

MONA HING: No trouble I have plenty of wind. Everyone
tells me so.

IDA BRAMBLE: Really –

*MONA stops and deflates the rubber ring cushion.
It makes some very amusing noises that MONA laughs
at. IDA grabs the ring from MONA.*

Would you stop doing that! You're making a scene in
public.

MOAN HING: You worry too much about what others think.
So what if I'm making a noise?

It's a public place, it's a free country, isn't it?

IDA BRAMBLE: Sssh!
Please stop it. If you stop it, I'll tell you why I'm here every Tuesday and Thursday.

Pause.

Promise.

She extends her hand to MONA – they shake. She gives back the inflatable ring, MONA deflates it quickly but noisily.

MONA HING: So sorry lady. Carry on.

IDA BRAMBLE: If we're going to do this then let's do it properly. Hello I'm Ida Bramble, Mrs.

MONA HING: Hello Ida Bramble, Mrs.
Hing Mona, but in this country, it's back to front.
Mona Hing, Mrs too. Though he's long gone.
I miss him still, but each day it's more of a struggle to remember his face.
I try putting on my glasses, my children often tell me to, so I can see better, but even this does not help.
See what did I say –

Taps her forehead.

Like a butterfly, never still long enough.

IDA BRAMBLE: Nice to meet you Mrs. Hing.

MONA HING: Mona, call me Mona.
Mrs. Hing makes me feel defective, like when you sit in front of the benefits people.

IDA BRAMBLE: I know that feeling.

They laugh.

MONA HING: So why do you sit on this bench Mrs. Angry Bramble?

IDA BRAMBLE: Call me Ida, just plane Ida.
I have that problem too – memory – picturing all the people who have passed /

MONA HING: Passed what?

IDA BRAMBLE: You know, moved on, passed away.

MONA gives IDA a look.

Died.

MONA HING: Why don't you say so?
You people are so afraid of death, you won't even give it its proper name.
You dance around the fire, but you know what, if you dance too close you end up falling into the flames!

IDA BRAMBLE: That's a very colourful way of putting things!

MONA HING: I'll shut up now and let you get edge ways in.

MONA smiles.

IDA BRAMBLE: Thank you, Mona.
I'm not very good at this talking malarkey.

MONA HING: Overrated. Sorry I'm shutting my mouth down now.

IDA BRAMBLE: It's funny – well it's not really – but that's the expression we use isn't it? 'It's funny...'
When really, we mean it's sad, tragic, or just plain bloody awful.
When Henry died, my husband, I wanted to die with him.
It was like having half of my body amputated.
Henry wasn't just a husband.
He was a father, a friend, my lifeline.
He served you know in the Far East.
Henry was actually stationed in Hong Kong, he left about a week before Hong Kong fell to the Japanese.

MONA HING: Terrible times, dark times.

Sam, my husband, he was a soldier too. He packed
me and the babies off to Britain, a month before the
Japanese took Hong Kong. We were probably on
one of the last ships out back to Britain before the
Japanese invaded.
I was so angry with Sam, I couldn't understand why
he was sending us away.

Beat.

I was a young, silly, immature woman, a girl really, not
like the girls now. Showing legs up to here, so brazen
no sense /
That's how I ended up in Blighty.

IDA BRAMBLE: Maybe Sam and Henry served together?

MONA HING: Not unless he was a Gangjiu or Dongjiang /

IDA BRAMBLE: The guerrillas.

MONA HING: *(Eyes wide.)* You know about the Hong
Kong guerrillas?

IDA BRAMBLE: Unsung heroes they fought tooth and nail
all the way through. So, your husband was a guerrilla,
a little devil.

MONA HING: Sam was always a trouble-maker. He was
the boy that always got into trouble. He was the boy
that lit firecrackers when he wasn't supposed to.
Who climbed walls and trees to pick fruit that wasn't
his – he called it farming!

IDA BRAMBLE: Sounds like a real character.
Henry was similar in many ways. He ended up as part
of the SOE operations.

He was a risk-taker too, so it was only a matter
of time before his luck ran out. A mixture of risky
operations and just bad luck parachuting into an area
of China that was pro-Japanese. He spent the rest of
the war after Black Christmas held by the Japanese.

First at Woosung then at a variety of other camps, finally ending up in Pingfang. He was never the same. I got him back, but not all of him.

MONA HING: Pingfang a cursed place. Even the birds will not fly over that place. It's like the death camps in Poland and Germany. Birds will not fly anywhere near.

IDA BRAMBLE: He never talked about any of it.
He had night terrors for seven months after he got home. Henry talked in his sleep too – we always used to joke that he'd be a rubbish spy.
I learnt a lot about the war, what he'd really had to endure.
'It's war, old girl. That's all that needs to be said. Let it go.'
I never could, let it go that is, maybe if I'd served...
I've come across many veterans who to this day are still haunted by the ghosts and demons of that war. Either they can't let go or it won't let them go.

MONA HING: Sam spent all those years fighting the Japanese back home, but in the end he couldn't settle down. Everywhere he saw the shadows of the Japanese occupation. Hong Kong was never the same for him. Sam left and came over to Britain to join me and the family.

IDA BRAMBLE: I come here and I sit on this bench and I remember.
I look at the memorial and it gives me some comfort. I remember those that fought and fell.
Those that fought and lived, though often I think that part of them fell with their comrades. I try to think of happier times. I close my eyes and I put the pieces of Henry's face together. But you're right, it's getting harder. It's like an old jigsaw puzzle, each year more pieces go missing.

Pause.

My children are grown up and have moved away.

They wanted to move me into an old people's home
and sell the house.
That's when I became angry and I just couldn't stop
being angry.
If it wasn't my children trying to institutionalise me,
it's cuts to my widows pension or questions about my
war pension /

MONA HING: Don't get me started.
I've been fighting for years to get the full war widows
pension. I'm told since Sam was not a white British
solider, I'm not entitled. I only get half or whatever
fraction it is. They have no feelings.
No respect or memory for what people have given to
Britain.

IDA BRAMBLE: That's terrible!
I'm so sorry, I had no idea.

MONA HING: Why are you apologising? It's not your fault.
We're strange little yellow people, isn't that what
Prince Edinburgh said?
We don't count. Our sacrifice is not good enough for
some.
I was walking through the Island last week /

IDA BRAMBLE: The Island?

MONA HING: Ah! You're a North Londoner, or maybe
Westminster lady, eh?

IDA BRAMBLE: How did you know?
Islington actually, I'd love to live in Westminster /

MONA HING: You me both!
Me for the Chinese supermarkets and maybe the odd
game of mah jong.
Why do you want to live in Westminster?

IDA BRAMBLE: The parks, the theatres, the galleries,
always something to do within walking distance.

MONA HING: The Island – the Isle of Dogs.

I was wearing a poppy for Remembrance Day, for Sam and all the others.

Ugly rude bald man came at me shouting.

Couldn't understand what he was shouting.

But he was very angry, shaking his fist.

Vein pumping on the side of his neck, making his face go lobster pink.

He lunges for me, I thought he was going to punch me.

He rips off my poppy saying I don't have the right to wear a poppy and that I'm a bad person.

No one stopped to help me.

I tried to talk to the lobster-faced man but he stormed off.

I picked up the broken poppy but it was no good, I couldn't undo the damage.

It made me so sad and so angry.

IDA BRAMBLE: It's no good being old in modern times. People don't like to be reminded where they've come from.

MONA HING: Lady Ida that's a deep true thought.

Pause.

So, you come here every Tuesday and Thursday to remember your Henry. You only remember Henry on Tuesdays and Thursdays? What are you remembering on Mondays, Wednesdays and Fridays?

IDA BRAMBLE: *(Laughs.)* I barely know you Mona, you're different to most of the people I know...

MONA HING: Course I am. How many Chinese OAPs do you know?

IDA BRAMBLE: None, well, one now.

Beat.

I come here on Tuesdays and Thursdays to avoid the home help and my grown-up children, whom I no longer recognise.

MONA HING: Dodging the long-nosed busy bodies.
I relate.

Pause.

What do you do in bad weather?
You can't sit our here in the rain and snow, it's not good for your health. And it's also stupid.

IDA BRAMBLE: I used to go into the café – but it closed down.
They're turning it into a Starbucks!
I suppose I'd go to the library.
At least I can see the memorial from the window.

MONA HING: You like to eat?

IDA BRAMBLE: Who doesn't /

MONA HING: You'd be surprised.
My children are big, they too have left home.
All they do now is feed my grandchildren Nando's or McDonald's.
They don't want home cooking; my grandchildren tell me it 'so gay'.
I don't associate with men like that. I have nothing against them.
I don't know anybody who is gay, except Raymond he does my hair, very polite and respectful.
Then they tell me it doesn't mean that, it means old-fashioned, uncool.
I look at my two grandchildren, sniggering and I know it means more than that.
Old ways, traditions change, or we'll end up like museum people.
So, do you like to eat Lady Ida?

IDA BRAMBLE: Yes, I do.

I miss the dinners Henry and I used to cobble together.
Stuffed vine leaves and salt egg soup /

MONA HING: How do you know about salt egg soup!

IDA BRAMBLE: Hong Kong.
Dumplings, noodles, bak choi, char siu.
Roast beef, spam hash, Yorkshire puddings and
steamed fish.

MONA HING: You have mixed taste.
I like it.
I like talking to you.

Beat.

First proper conversation I've had in years.
Lady Ida I have to go now.
You take care of yourself.
You got a piece of paper?

IDA rummages around in her pockets.

Will this do?

IDA hands MONA an envelope.

MONA HING: Champion, as Sam would have said.

MONA finds a pen and writes on the back.

I'm not modern I don't have a mobile phone.
I don't want my children following me around all day
and night.
I have proper phone at home.
You ring me any Tuesday or Thursday when the
weather is bad.
I'll take you in and we can both look out the window
through the rain at the memorial.
Maybe I'll even teach you how to cook proper food
and play mah jong.
Or maybe I'll just meet you on the bench here and we
will both sit and remember together.

IDA BRAMBLE: I'd like that, I really would.

MONA HING: Lady Ida, don't think too long it's getting late and the moon is bleeding and swollen. Not good for us to be out late these days.
Ok for chickens to run around, but us donkeys we need to be indoors.
Bye, bye.

MONA walks away at a surprising speed leaving IDA alone on the bench.

IDA BRAMBLE: Well Henry that was a breath of... something. I'd better go love. Mona was right it's getting late.
I'll be back soon you take care and wrap up well.

IDA gets up and walks slowly away she stops and stares at the blood red moon.

IDA BRAMBLE: Extraordinary moon, never seen one like that before, wonder if it means anything –

IDA walks slowly off into the distance.

BLACKOUT.

HOSPITAL ICU

JACKIE lies awake staring at the blood red moon.

JACKIE: Mum used to say don't fall asleep with the moon
shining on your face, don't point at the moon your ears
will fall off –
A blood red moon means turbulent times ahead.
It's already started.

There is a knock on the door – MR. CHAN walks in.

Dad?!

*MR. CHAN sits down next to his son's bed. JACKIE reaches
out to to take his father's hand. MR. CHAN removes his
hand out of reach.*

Whatever it is, say it and then leave.

MR. CHAN: I would cut you off like I would cut of an
infected limb. But your mother – I have brought some
of your things. The rest you can arrange to pick up
later. I have set up an allowance account for you.
Here are the keys to the old flat.

He throws some keys onto the bed.

It is yours, do what you like with it.
If you go to university I will support you further.
I hope that your wounds heal quickly.

MR. CHAN turns to leave.

JACKIE: That's it?

MR. CHAN: You have brought this on yourself.

Beat.

You disgust me /

JACKIE: Why, what did I do that was so /

MR. CHAN: You have broken the ancestral line.

JACKIE: Please don't turn your back on me. Dad!

MR. CHAN leaves without turning back. JACKIE starts to cough again.

What's the point – of any of this!

JACKIE has another coughing fit – staring at the blood red moon.

To Mum a blood red moon was a bad omen.

Beat.

I don't want to be on my own – the one thing I had was family –

JACKIE drags himself out of bed. He uses the drip stand for support. He shuffles towards the window, finds the door to the balcony. He walks out onto the balcony, slumps onto a chair and stares at the blood red moon.

CHU appears.

JACKIE: This can't be good – no offence, but aren't you dead?

CHU: The saddest thing is the death of the heart.

JACKIE: I'm hallucinating – /

CHU: Southerners do not dream about camels and northerners do not dream about elephants /

JACKIE: You sound like my mum /

CHU: You do not dream about women, but your father dreams of grandchildren –

JACKIE: Something like that /

CHU: You spoke to my wife, that was kind.

JACKIE: I've never spoken to a dead person before.

CHU: Does it count if you're dead and you're speaking to
yourself?

JACKIE: I guess –
I don't see why not /

CHU: I am tethered to this place –
Li would say that I'm trying to scrape the moon from
the bottom of the sea.
I lack restrictions but I can do nothing, merely observe.

JACKIE: And what do you observe Mr. Chu?

CHU: That I loved but I let go –

JACKIE: That I let go before I loved –

CHU: I spent my life bowed over, worrying about things
that were unimportant, hiding myself from the world.
Muttering that I was part of it. But you cannot be part
of something that you do not contribute to.
Don't be like me, don't waste your breath and energy
lying to yourself. Don't be afraid to speak out.

*CHU vanishes JACKIE is alone on the balcony staring at
the blood red moon.*

JACKIE: It would be so easy just to step out onto the air
and fall.

BLACKOUT.

IT'S A WONDERFUL WOK AND THE HOSPITAL MORGUE

LI sits in the semi-dark. CHU sits in the morgue.

LI: Looking out of the window at the blood red moon everything is pouring down so hard –
It's only been a few hours but those hours have brushed past me like years.

CHU: You don't have to stay on any more wife. You're free to travel /

LI: I'll see you safely into the ground and then –

CHU: You'll need help, why don't you take on that young man who comes in with his –

Beat.

Friend.

LI: I wonder how that young man is – his parents must have been out of their minds with worry – I've seen him grow up from school to college. I never asked his name. We nodded to his parents, we smiled but we didn't speak. What I would give to be annoyed by the squeaking hatch and the spitting fryer that you promised to get fixed but never did. You thought that I didn't know. I knew you were fixing things – badly – oh Chu.

CHU: And I thought I had fooled you!
Do not anxiously hope for that which has not yet come; do not vainly regret what has already passed.

LI: Will gather up your things and put them in the bedroom and then close the door. After that – what then?

BLACKOUT.

THE CHAN'S HOME

MRS. CHAN is crying silently. She sits in the semi-dark in the dining room looking out of the the French door windows at the blood red moon. MR. CHAN walks in, he observes his wife for a second or two.

MR. CHAN: It is done.

Beat.

We should take that break, the one you are always trying to make me take. We could go to Scotland /

MRS. CHAN: I don't want to go to Scotland. I want to see my son /

MR. CHAN slams his hand down hard onto the table, MRS. CHAN flinches.

I want to see my son!

MR. CHAN: You cannot see what you do not have!

MRS. CHAN: Just as you cannot hold onto what you have thrown away /

MR. CHAN: You walk out of this house you cannot re-enter it.

MRS. CHAN: Yes I know.

MRS. CHAN picks up a small suitcase and walks out of the dining room. MR. CHAN stands in the gloom, we hear the front door open and shut.

BLACKOUT.

PUBLIC PARK WAR MEMORIAL

IDA BRAMBLE is sat on the bench staring at the war memorial.

IDA BRAMBLE: Henry are you there?

Beat.

I was nearly home. Just rounding the last corner and – there they all were. Draped over their cars, leaning up against the gate post, sat on the porch. Heads buried, eyes glued to their screens, thumbs, tip-tapping.
I wasn't in the mood for another family intervention. After the fussing and tutting it always comes back to, 'We worry about you Mum, if you'd only move into a home, where it's safe. Staff on call to help you...'
More like to interfere.
I came back here. I thought I can grab a coffee at Niccos – I'd forgotten he's shut down. So I came back here to talk to you, Henry I'm so tired, tired all the time and cold. Do you mind my dear, I'm just going to shut my eyes for a few minutes.

I almost expected to see Mona, the lady I met this afternoon. She told me to go home, that people like us shouldn't be out late at night. Oh Henry do you remember the dances we used to go to and how late we used to stay out. I just can't seem to keep my eyes open.

IDA drifts off.

MONA appears pushing a battered shopping trolley loaded with goods. MONA marches past the bench. Stops and reverses until she is next to the bench looking at IDA.

MONA HING: It's Lady Ida.

Peers at IDA and sits down heavily next to her on the bench.

Shouldn't be sleeping out in the cold, it's not good for you, is it Sam?
I told you to go home it's not safe out here –
I should be getting on, I have to put all these supplies away.

MONA reaches out and pulls the shopping trolley towards her. She spots something in the cart and lets out a scream – IDA stirs.

IDA BRAMBLE: Mona! I was hoping I'd bump into you again /

MONA HING: Stupid people how many times do I have to tell them? I don't eat char siu bun. It brings back bad memories – people did terrible things during the war in Hong Kong to survive –

Turns to look at IDA.

What are you doing out here like a down and out!

IDA BRAMBLE: I was resting my eyes /

MONA HING: While you were resting your eyes Lady Ida, your nose was talking /

IDA BRAMBLE: What are you implying /

MONA HING: Implying? Not implying, just saying /

IDA BRAMBLE: Well I resent /

MONA HING: Lady you snore!

Pause.

I'm so tired Lady Ida, tired of – all this, come on let's get out of the cold. You come back with me, I cook you a proper meal /

IDA BRAMBLE: I thought the Chinese looked after their own, why aren't your children looking after you?

MONA HING: Yes, all Chinese people exactly the same. We all huddle together in one dwelling and love each other to bits. Where did you get that piece of knowledge, Chinese People for Dummies? People are people, good, bad, stupid, indifferent doesn't matter what colour.

Pause.

I'm out here for the same reason you are Lady Ida, family is a pain in the arse. My children drive me mad, want to put me in a home, they say it's for my own protection!

Pools of light come up on It's A Wonderful Wok, the hospital ICU, the morgue and the public park bench.

The remainder of the action until the end is done split stage. All locations are visible to the audience. Dialogue that appears in symmetrical columns is spoken at the same time. For dialogue that appears asymmetrically the usual rules occur: one person speaks after another, the person on the left speaks first.

IT'S A WONDERFUL WOK	THE MORGUE
LI: When you first set this business up we constantly talked about making enough so that we could go back home.	
	CHU: How we argued – like a good married couple /
LI: This is our home – where else would I go?	
	CHU: A lifetime of toil –
LI: It's not that I'm not capable /	
	CHU: You're capable.

LI: Do I want to live alone,
    surrounded by people who
    don't want me here?

> **CHU:** The palace leads
>   to fame, the market
>   to fortune, and
>   loneliness to wisdom.

LI: This loneliness and separation
    will break me.

HOSPITAL ICU SIDE WARD

JACKIE lies in bed staring at the blood red moon.

JACKIE: In a city of 8.6 million but I might as well be
    Robinson Crusoe!

MRS. CHAN walks in with a suitcase.

MRS. CHAN: Hello Jian.

JACKIE: Mum – what, what are you doing here?

MRS. CHAN: Visiting my son.

JACKIE: Are you going somewhere?

MRS. CHAN: Yes. I'm going to see the ocean.

JACKIE: Any one in particular?

*MRS. CHAN kisses JACKIE on the forehead and leaves.
JACKIE carefully gets up from the bed and walks out onto
the balcony, sits down and stares at the blood red moon.*

JACKIE: I *feel* the same as everyone else, the shock
    comes when you find that you're not. We are all the
    same under the skin, they say –
    Even if I could turn myself outside in, would it make
    any difference?

LI: We're supposed to count
our blessings. Be grateful for
our comfortable lives.
We should have been safe in
this country, we should have
been protected. My husband
should never have died /

CHU: Happiness is like
a sunbeam, which
the last shadow
intercepts, while
adversity is as often
as the rain of spring –

LI: They treated us like criminals
as if we were the wrongdoers –
as if we were somehow
responsible for what was
happening to us – that our
'being' caused people to react
in a violent way and it was not
their fault but ours because of
who we were! At one point – do
you remember – they told us to
shut up shop and move
somewhere else /

CHU: To open a shop is
easy, to keep a shop
open, that is an art /

LI: To keep a shop open, that is
an art. I can hear you so clearly
saying that. Standing quietly in
the door way looking at me –
with long suffering patience –

CHU: Quiet thoughts
mend the body /

LI: What if I don't want to be
mended, I just want it all to
stop, I want to be anywhere
but here – at the same time
I can't bring myself to leave.

> **CHU:** People are the
> root of any community.
> And food is its first
> necessity.

LI: If I leave – I have nothing, the
shouters, the haters have won.
They succeed, they rip from my
hands and heart everything I
have ever known or loved –

> **CHU:** Things at the
> worst will mend.

LI: If I stay I will have to look into
the eyes of my tormentors
every single day, I don't know if
I can do that –

> **CHU:** Learn to be
> content with what
> you have, and you
> will be a happy soul.

LI: I don't know anything else –
everything here is like an exposed
nerve. I touch a handle, memory
explodes and the pain of you not
being here grows. The empty
space that you should fill grows–

> **CHU:** Our hearts are
> forever tied.

LI: Our life was bitterly short /

CHU: I died without too many regrets. My love is as deep as the sea and as tender as water.

LI: Looking up at the blood red moon. With my hands I hold, together we will grow old.

CHU: In the sky, may we be two birds flying side by side. On earth, may we be be two branches inseparably tied.

CHU slowly lies back down on the morgue trolley.

LI: As the bright moon shines over the sea, from far away you share this moment with me.

LI gets up, switches on the lights and starts to clear up to get ready for business.

JACKIE: *(JACKIE is still sitting out on the the balcony.)* It would be so easy to step out onto the air. *(Stands up and walks towards the balcony railing.)*

MONA HING: *(MONA and IDA on bench. MONA looks at IDA, she's nodded off. IDA snores. MONA nudges IDA, she stirs.)* Lady Ida you're snoring again. You got sleeping sickness?

JACKIE: To free fall into blackout

IDA BRAMBLE: It's turned a bit chilly hasn't it? Well, it is late isn't it? /

JACKIE: Everything. Joy, happiness, disappointment, despair, shame, loneliness. All falls in on itself into that rushing black hole /

MONA HING: It's not late, we only think that it's late because we're old. Only eleven o'clock, that's the time the young ones are getting ready to go out – remember?

JACKIE: *(Climbs up onto the balcony railing.)* No more worries, no more secrets, no more – nothing but black peace –

IDA BRAMBLE: How did I get to be so old, so quickly /

MONA HING: You are coming home with me for some home cooking.

LI continues to prep.

CHU covers himself with a sheet.

JACKIE: *(Spreads his arms out and removes drip.)* I can fly –

MONA HING: *(Gets up and stretches.)* Come on Lady Ida time to go home.

IDA BRAMBLE: Yes I suppose it is, you'll have to point me in the right direction for the tube or bus.

JACKIE takes one foot off the railing and dangles it over the edge.

MONA HING: You old and deaf? I said you are coming home with me.

LI: Will change the name of the shop tomorrow... Ma Chu's.

IDA BRAMBLE: So you did.

MONA HING: Ready?

IDA stands up.

LI: *(Switches on the sign.)* It's time...

JACKIE: *(Walks off the balcony.)* I'm flying

(Grabs trolley and IDA.) Let's go.

(LI turns sign to OPEN and looks up at the moon.) Chu this is going to be the best bloody takeaway this side of –

JACKIE falls.

JACKIE looks at the moon.

MONA and IDA start to walk away.

CHU sighs.

LI: *(The phone rings, LI picks up.)* It's A Won... Ma Chu's...

Come on Lady Ida.

LI: No we're open as ususal...

IDA BRAMBLE: Wait
for me then...

LI: Thank you...
It's been renamed...

MONA HING: It's cold
and my bladder wants
to get home /

LI: Yes in memory of
my husband...

IDA BRAMBLE: Too
much information /

LI: Yes thank you...
Now what would
you like to order...

MONA HING: Happy
to share, that's just
who I am.

LI: Chicken with
lemon...

JACKIE: Free

MONA and IDA walk off.

*The blood red moon grows and It's A Wonderful Wok
neon lights flicker and then go dark.*

THE END.

Lucy Chau Lai-Tuen was born and orphaned on the Crown Colony of Hong Kong. She was exported to the UK in the late fifties as a transracial adoptee – 1 of 106 that were the first ever group of government sanctioned and organised transracial adoptees to the UK.

Lucy is an actor, published poet, filmmaker and playwright. As a writer Lucy has been writing professionally since 2011. Her first play (a solo theatre piece) *There Are Two Perfectly Good Me's: One dead the other unborn* was produced by True Heart Theatre and performed by Lucy in November 2011 at the New Diorama Theatre as part of a mini season of solo theatre pieces by female writers from the global Chinese diaspora.

Since then Lucy has been commissioned by Nimble Fish Arts for the Re:Play bursary to write *Ungrateful*, a solo theatre piece which was performed by Lucy at Poetry International 2015 on The Southbank. Other work includes: *Restrain Your Grief and Adapt to the Mishap* (Royal Court for Live Lunch Hidden), Come to Where I'm From: London (Paines Plough/Tamasha TC), Commonword (The Black and Asian Writers Conference 2016), and *Thursday's Child Has Far To Go*. Lucy's work also appeared in the first ever published anthology of flash fiction by BAME writers and will appear again this year in a second anthology.

A collection of Lucy's poetry *Ungrateful - A Paper Daughter* was published in the Spring, 2017 by an independent US publishing house.

THE CONFESSION
by CATHY SK LAM

Production History

The Confession was first performed as part of Foreign Goods Last Forever 2: Visions Of England at Theatre503, London on the 24th and 25th April 2017 with the following cast and creative team:

Cast
Charlotte Chiew

Creative Team
Writer   Cathy SK Lam
Director   Bethany Kapila
Producer   Jingan Young

SHIELA: I have a confession to make.

Long silence.

I only date guys who are rich, well-educated, driven, smart, white, like very white, the older the better, the balder the better. I despise my own kind, who are so very Asian that we share the same values and culture. So that I can brag about all these interracial dating experiences with my own kind, and dismay them with all of the amazing things they have missed, and yes that does make me a shallow minded gold digger.

The best part is, I will get a new passport, American is the best, but I will consider European and Australian rather than the British... I know what you are thinking, but Theresa May hates me. Together we can make Britain a country that works for everyone. Woah! That's...really Interesting. No judgement here, I am an Asian, I am very respectful to everyone. Trump hates me too, but luckily my last name is not Kim, and he looks up to Xi for his extraordinary elevation.

There is Chinese slang that describes us Asians as '食洋腸 既女人' (pronounced: Sik Yeung Cheung Ge Lui Yan). 'The woman who enjoys Western sausage.' Well... I don't mind at all, if you have dim sum long enough, spaghetti can be a good alternative. Us Chinese are very serious, yet very causal at the same time about what we eat. We eat everything, we don't have everything. A very serious eating guide is what we need.

Long silence.

'Asians all look the same!'

'Oh, never mind! So do you sweetie! I can never tell if you are Dutch, German or British.'

Some people think that I am Thai, Indonesian, Malaysian, Singaporean, Japanese, Korean and finally Chinese!

Do you know how they try to guess? 'Sa-waii-di-ca', 'Kon-ni-chi-wa', 'An-nyeong-ha-se-yo', 'Ni Hao', 'Nei Ho', usually people will find triumph if they think that they've figured they can greet you in your language...well sort of...and will request a high five for pronouncing your exotic Asian name correctly. I don't mind...but where is my high five if I pronounce your name 'Peter' correctly? This is so unfair, so is the world.

I figured that people always love giving us limit tests.

'You got an A in your calculus class, right? It's probably because Chinese people are just naturally good at math.'

'I probably drive better than you, 'cause you are Chinese, and a woman.'

'Do you know Jackie Chan? Jet Lee? Lee Ann maybe? Are they the only famous Chinese celebrities? Oh, I know one more, Bruce Lee, have you practiced Kung Fu...yahhhhhh!...'

'Please don't have me taking my shoes off before entering your house.'

'Hey hun, can you calculate this tip? You are Chinese.'

'Ok la, we are going to this la. Also la, do this la. No la...lalalalalalalala.'

'How come your mum always smiles at me and does not talk to me?'

'Well, China still has child labour, right? You must have been through a lot...'

And that doesn't annoy me at all, I LOVE it!

The blank look on my face doesn't necessarily mean that I am mad. I am Chinese and I am very calm, that's the beauty of Chinese Zen. We love peace. Peace is gold. We are very good diplomats; the world loves us. No one understands better peace than us.

Social order and harmony is way too important...
We are the perfect successor of Confucius, and
we unswervingly follow the path of peaceful
development. The ultimate goal for the Chinese!

Therefore, filial piety is very important to us. We must
show devotion and obedience to our parents, and also
to our ancestors. We must involve ourselves in every
aspect of our kids' lives. This is how we show concern
for our families. This is LOVE. Our gracious leader Xi
encourages us to be willing to promote the long-term,
healthy and stable development of bilateral relations
on the basis of mutual respect and mutual benefits.
So, if I meet my perfect white guy, I will build a family
with him immediately, so I can intervene in his life with
proper reason. And no one, NO ONE will be able to
intervene with *our* internal affairs. I can't see our world
together if he is an outsider, everything is way easier if
you are in the same circle. Everything done inside the
same circle, under the table.

Then last but not the least, let's build our face
together, never forget an individual's success and
shame belongs to the whole family! So, world, I am
ready to rumble just like Xi! I am going to take care of
you, you and you.

Grins.

I don't come and cause you headaches, what more is
there to be said?

Hmmm, I am...submissive, obedient, loyal, quiet, easy,
exotic, tiny and cute. I look just like one of your exes,
who was also Chinese.

So yes, I love dating white guys, because they think
that we are just THE cutest little Asian girls that will do
everything for them. Such a promising relationship.

Long silence.

I have a confession to make.

Cathy SK Lam is Artistic Director of ThreeWoods Playwright.

She joined Theatre Horizon (Hong Kong) in 2007, as the company manager and was appointed as the Executive Director later. During her time in Theatre Horizon, she has performed and produced numerous plays including *Can't Play Won't Play* by Dario Fo, *Winds Of Change, I AM HAPPY* (One Man Show), and *French Kiss*.

In 2011 she received Emerging Artists Project Grant from Hong Kong Arts Development Council and established ThreeWoods Playwright. She created and produced *Revelation Of Love, Every Little Thing, Bon Voyage, Shi Yi, The Curious Incident of A Little Girl, Solitaire, All About Ruby*, and five star plays *The Immigration Lottery, Wither On the Wine* and *Smoking With Grandma*.

Follow her Instagram: cathylamsk

THE SWING
by TAN SUET LEE

Production History

The Swing had its first full dramatised read at Centre 42, Singapore on the 1st May 2017 with the follwoing cast and creative team:

Cast

Jalyn Han
Chanel Chan
Audrey Luo
Rei Poh
Julie Wee

Creative Team

Writer	Tan Suet Lee
Director	Liting Tan
Producer	Jean Tay, Saga Seed Theatre
Dramaturg	Marcia Vanderstraaten

Extracts of *The Swing* were presented at Theatre503, London, November 2016 and at La MaMa, New York, January 2014.

Characters

MEI SUN – Chinese, 30

SHIRLEY – Mei Sun's daughter, 8 and mid 30s

POPO – Mei Sun's mother, late 60s

RONG YIN – Mei Sun's brother, 40

AH JUN – Rong Yin's wife, 30s

DIRECTOR – Caucasian, 30s
played by same actor as Rong Yin

DELIVERY MAN – Chinese, 40s
played by same actor as Rong Yin

Setting

Popo's house in a kampong (village) in Singapore
Shirley's high rise apartment in Shanghai

Time

1973
1976
Present day

Prologue

PRESENT

On stage there are three spaces with three identical wrought iron swings. The kind commonly found in gardens in South East Asia. POPO's swing is green. MEI SUN's swing is also green. SHIRLEY's swing is black and there is a blue cloth loosely thrown on it.

Lights up on SHIRLEY's swing in her apartment in Shanghai. There are boxes stacked high all around.

SHIRLEY: You can't leave it here. You have to take it away.

DELIVERY MAN: *(Mandarin.)* I don't understand.

SHIRLEY: *(At the swing.)* This. It has to go.

DELIVERY MAN: *(Mandarin.)* I see your mouth moving but I don't know what's coming out.

SHIRLEY: What?

DELIVERY MAN: *(Mandarin.)* You are Chinese. Why can't you speak Chinese (Putonghua)? Stupid girl.

SHIRLEY: Wait.

Grabs a copy of her Conversational Mandarin, flicks through it.

Say it again. But this time more slowly. I can't catch the words if you go too fast.

DELIVERY MAN: *(Mandarin – slowly.)* Y-o-u a-r-e s-t-u-p-i-d.

SHIRLEY: *(Flicks through her Conversational Mandarin, again.)* No. Can't find it.

DELIVERY MAN: *(Mandarin, with invoice in hand.)* What's your name?

SHIRLEY: *(Flicks through her Conversational Mandarin, again.)* Yes, I know this one. Wait a minute. Here we are.

Wo shi......no...how do you say it...wo jiao...wo jiao ming shi... Shirley Tan...

Delivery man shows her the invoice.

DELIVERY MAN: *(Mandarin.)* Correct. And this is your name. And this is your delivery.

SHIRLEY: *(Flicks through her Conversational Mandarin, again.)* No. Bu. Bu.

Fuck it. Look. I know it's got my name on the invoice. But that swing is not mine. There must be some mistake.

You have to remove it.

Fuck. Fuck. Fuck.

DELIVERY MAN: *(Mandarin.)* Western educated women. Mouths like sewers. No manners. My daughter would never speak like that.

SHIRLEY: Fifty bloody boxes stacked like lego. Do you understand? I don't have space for this in my 300 foot studio apartment. *(Checks the book again.)* Ming bai?

DELIVERY MAN: *(Mandarin.)* Sorry, lady. This is your problem not mine.

(In broken English.) You have nice day. Bye Bye.

He exits.

SHIRLEY: Hey wait, wait you can't go. Shit.

God, I wish I'd gone to those bloody Mandarin classes in Soho.

SHIRLEY gets up and starts to undo a couple of boxes, but her eyes keep going back to the swing. She eyes it suspiciously.

I'll call Mum. Maybe she knows something.

Hello? Hailsham retirement village? Hi. I wonder if I could speak to Ms Mei Sun Tan. Mei...M...E...I...S...U... what? Say that again?

What? When?... Do you know where she is? Do you have a number? Alright I'll call back on Monday. Thank you. Fuck.

She moves to the swing. Finds it uncomfortable. Moves the blue cloth on the swing to create space. Then she sees it – a letter taped to the underside of the swing. She reads it.

AH JUN: Dearest Shirley, I write to tell you...

Lights up on POPO and MEI SUN's swings. POPO is peeling a basket of bean sprouts. MEI SUN sings a Hakka song – 'Bright Moonlight' (Ngiet gong gong).

Act One

SCENE 1 – HOME COMING

POPO: I like to sing
Old women like to sing
We sing to remember
To hear our ancestors
Carry their voices
Over hills and high mountains.

We sing to remember the dry earth
Hard soil, hot sun
Empty wells, unripe tapioca
Small packets of red tobacco.

Children drowned at sea
Husbands taken by other women
Daughters given to distant lands.

MEI SUN: *(Read as if remembering a script.)* Our road has no exit. It's a cul-de sac. We have a garden with a swing. In the summer, roses grow and in the winter, frost crunches beneath our feet.

I take the number 70 bus to the hospital. My uniform is blue and I wear a cap. The sister-in-charge smokes, but never in front of the patients. Shirley starts school at 9am and finishes at 3pm. She is a good student. She has many friends and is never bullied. Every day after school she has a cup of milk and two chocolate biscuits. On Sundays we visit my mother-in-law. She lives by the sea. We eat roast beef, potatoes, and peas, and have bread and butter pudding for dessert.

Yes, I am very lucky.

She looks at her watch and then shouts out to SHIRLEY.

Shirley?

Shirley?

Lights up on SHIRLEY and her swing. The boxes have now been cleared. SHIRLEY is seven years old, and lying face down on the swing, her finger traces imaginary pictures.

SHIRLEY: Yessss?

MEI SUN: Are you done yet?

SHIRLEY: No...

MEI SUN: Why not?

SHIRLEY: I sound silly. It's like I'm telling lies.

MEI SUN: I told you. It's not lies. It's like playing pretend. It's a – story, like *Snow White and the Seven Dwarfs*, or *Beauty and the Beast*.

If you learn your lines I'll buy you a Kit Kat at the airport. Okay?

Two Kit Kats?

Three Kit Kats and a packet of Rolos? My final offer.

Be a good girl. Let's hear it.

SHIRLEY: On Sundays, we go to my grandmother's house. I call her Nana. My Nana likes to sit...

MEI SUN: Sew...she likes to sew on her sewing machine... carry on.

SHIRLEY: She makes cushion covers.

MEI SUN: For?

SHIRLEY: Christmas and Easter.

On some days...

MEI SUN: What?

SHIRLEY: When there are no stars in the sky...

MEI SUN: *(Warning.)* Shirley...

SHIRLEY: Her face is like the moon and...

(Spoken really fast.) You see her fat warts. And when she's really hungry she puts tomato ketchup on baby kittens and eats them for a midnight snack.

MEI SUN: Do you want me to get the wooden spoon?

SHIRLEY gets up and starts running around her swing as if she is being chased.

SHIRLEY: Nooo...

Help...somebody save me.

Okay. I'll be good.

On Sundays we go to my grandmother's house. I call her Nana. She lives in a...zoo and swims with humpback whales, and she loves me and I love her. The End.

MEI SUN gets up from her swing and chases SHIRLEY.

SCENE 2 – THESE ARE A FEW OF MY FAVOURITE THINGS

All three women are swinging on their swings. SHIRLEY speaks as a grown-up.

POPO: Eating nasi lemak with extra chili.

MEI SUN: Butterfly wings making footprints in the sand.

SHIRLEY: Defining and implementing organisational objectives.

POPO and MEI SUN look at SHIRLEY. She does a 'What?' gesture.

POPO: Drinking Johnnie Walker from a cup.

MEI SUN: The sun singing an aria to the cold.

SHIRLEY: Measuring corporate performance using effective key indicators.

POPO: Next door's ice kacang maker.

MEI SUN: Five small bicycles strung to a tap.

SHIRLEY: Jimmy Choos four inch stilettos.

POPO and MEI SUN nod approvingly.

POPO: When the wind dries my sarong on the washing line.

MEI SUN: Shifting marble slabs in open seas.

SHIRLEY: Friday night, cocktails at Benny's followed by a bloody good f...

POPO: *(Interrupts quickly.)* A nice clean altar table.

MEI SUN: Starlit waterfalls in a forest of pine.

SHIRLEY: I'm lost on that one. I don't know... I really don't know.

SCENE 3 – GETTING READY

POPO is asleep on the swing. The basket of plucked bean sprouts on the floor. RONG YIN carries two poles. He fits them on the upper frame of the swing. He returns with a big basket of wet clothes.

RONG YIN begins to hang the clothes on the pole above POPO's head. A drop of water drips on to her face.

POPO: Rain coming...quick...my towels, my cloths, my sarongs.

RONG YIN looks at her briefly and carries on hanging out the washing. POPO wakes with a start and realises she has been sleeping.

Aiyoh? Why never call me? What time is it?

RONG YIN: Four o'clock.

POPO: So late? So many things to do. Iron clothes, set hair, clean toilet...

POPO picks up the basket of bean sprouts and goes to leave.

You going like that is it?

Son, this is airport, not bus station, you know or not. Airport got many important people. Must comb hair, wear long sleeve, wear long pants. Let people see you are rich.

RONG YIN: But I'm not rich.

POPO: I know. You know. But they all don't know. Use your... *(Points to her head)*. Poor people only look. Rich people sit inside airplane.

Morning you go Ah Chong provision shop right?

He say anything?

RONG YIN: About what?

POPO: My party.

Saturday, at market, I tell everyone.

The background sound of a wet market, the sound of grating coconut.

I take the wooden box...the one they put watermelons, pomelos...

POPO stands on the swing.

I get four or five and put one on top on top like that *(she does the action)* and after I check steady, I stand tall, so everyone can see me, and I...*(she clears her throat)*...but Ah Choon grate coconut so loud, nobody can hear. So I say, 'Oi Ah Choon quiet five minute can?' *(The sound of grating coconut stops.)* Then I say:

Ah, hello everybody. Ah...you all know soon I will die right? *(The market sound goes quiet.)*

No need to be sad. We all know one day we must sit on lotus, and fly across river. But we must not be afraid. We must celebrate. We must sing and dance because after this, if we are good in life, we will be free.

So...next week I have a big party with lots of *makan* and you all invited.

The sound of clapping.

And...also you all can see my daughter Mei Sun. She is nurse in big English hospital. Got many patients. She come home in aeroplane with her daughter.

Yah, yah... I very happy to see my granddaughter. Next time she close her eyes, she can remember my face, then her prayers will be strong.

After I cross river, I will tell our ancestors she has fair skin and big eyes. I will tell them her father is *ang moh*... a doctor, with blue eyes. But dead already. Maybe they have seen him.

So next week, six o'clock, come, we eat nice food, sing nice song...one last time. Thank you. Thank you.

RONG YIN: You're not going to die Ma. The doctors...

POPO: I don't listen to doctors.

I listen to my bones.

Where's Ah Jun? My char siu pork ready?

So many things to do. Cut garlic, peel shallots. Your wife so useless.

Want to die also cannot. Next time dead, still must come back and chop chicken.

RONG YIN: Don't say that Ma...

POPO: Ah Jun?

Ah Jun?

She exits.

RONG YIN: *(RONG YIN puts on a fake English accent and speaks like an old English gentleman.)* Hello dear sister, how wonderful it is to see you. I do hope you and your offspring had a most agreeable flight. And that the roasted peanuts were to your satisfaction. I myself prefer to sit near the window so that I may see the wonderous lush landscape as we descend into Paya Lebar international airport.

And dear niece Shirley. I am your *tai koo* but you can call me Uncle Rong Yin or Uncle Charlie. That is what my friends at the community club call me.

I do hope you will enjoy your stay with us. Your grandmamma and I have been looking forward to your trip for a long while now. We will endeavor to make your stay with us as pleasant as possible, and if there is anything we can do to make your stay more comfortable please do not hesitate to let us know. Thank you.

AH JUN enters, clearly pregnant.

RONG YIN: Ma is looking for you.

AH JUN: Let her look. Crazy woman.

She ask why I never cook crab.

I tell her, you never buy, how to cook?

RONG YIN: Then go and buy.

AH JUN: How? My pockets already empty?

Crazy woman go and invite whole village. Like she is sultan or something.

People die every day. She is special. Must have party. I dare not show my face in any provision shops. All of them we owe credit.

RONG YIN: It's because of Mei Sun and her daughter. She wants to show them off.

AH JUN: Dying and still want to show off?

And your sister – thirteen years, we still never see a single cent.

RONG YIN: Shuush. Not so loud.

AH JUN: You promised me...

RONG YIN: I know.

AH JUN: You promised me.

RONG YIN: Okay. Okay.

AH JUN: So you ask her?

RONG YIN: I'll ask her. I'll ask her.

AH JUN: Good.

AH JUN pulls him onto the swing and places his hand on her belly.

We wait so long. Now, only two more months and baby will be here.

RONG YIN: Ah Mei is a nurse. She is earning well...

AH JUN: *(AH JUN sniffs disbelievingly.)* I see. Then I believe.

RONG YIN: When she give me back the money, you know the first thing I do?

I buy my wife a beautiful ruby necklace. How? My wife? You like?

AH JUN: Talk so big. One small crab cannot buy. Want to buy beautiful ruby necklace.

RONG YIN: Other people's stomach not important.

But a beautiful wife must wear beautiful things.

He goes to kiss her but she offers her cheek instead.

Why, so shy?

AH JUN: Everyone can see.

AH JUN nods at a passing neighbour, embarrassed.

RONG YIN: Let them see.

RONG YIN gets up and climbs on the back of the swing and gently pushes AH JUN. His face hidden by the washing.

Shall I compare thee to a summer's day?

AH JUN: Huh?

RONG YIN: Thou art more lovely and more temperate...

AH JUN: What?

RONG YIN: Rough winds do shake the darling buds of May,

And summer's lease hath all too short a date...

AH JUN: *(Waves to the neighbours and smiles uncomfortably.)* Ah Huat is looking.

RONG YIN: Sometime too hot the eye of heaven shines,

And often is his gold complexion dimm'd...

AH JUN: You look like a monkey. Wait you fall then you know.

RONG YIN: And every fair from fair sometime declines...

RONG YIN slips temporarily.

AH JUN: Ha! You see.

RONG YIN: By chance, or nature's changing course, untrimm'd,

But thy eternal summer shall not fade,

Nor lose possession of that fair thou ow'st,

Nor shall Death brag thou wander'st in his shade...

AH JUN: Gone 'xiao' (crazy) already.

RONG YIN: When in eternal lines to time thou grow'st,

So long as men can breathe, or eyes can see,

So long lives this, and this gives life to thee.

POPO: *(Off stage.)* Ah Jun.

Jun ah.

AH JUN walks off shaking her head, leaving RONG YIN swinging by himself.

SCENE 4 – AIRPORT

MEI SUN and SHIRLEY come in carrying bags. They walk through the swings, and in and around them as if they're in the airport showing tickets and passports etc. SHIRLEY eating a Kit Kat.

SHIRLEY: Mum why do we have so many soap bars? They smell horrible and my bag smells like a chemist

MEI SUN: They're gifts for friends and relatives. You have to bring something when you visit people. You can't go empty handed.

SHIRLEY: Why not? We always do here.

MEI SUN: It's different in Asia. They'll be expecting it.

They reach their swings and sit as if they are on the plane and strap themselves in.

Are you belted up?

Now watch the lady do her demonstration. It might save your life.

SHIRLEY: Isn't it like saying: 'Hello how are you? You smell really bad. Here's a bar of soap.'

MEI SUN: You don't realise how lucky we are to live in England. Scented soap, running water, supermarkets lined with tins of baked beans. You'll see what I mean when we get there.

Stop talking. We're taking off.

They push off on their swings.

SHIRLEY: Weeeeeeeeee.

SCENE 5 – THE SWING

MEI SUN and SHIRLEY 'unbuckle their seat belts' and walk towards POPO's swing. MEI SUN goes in the house. SHIRLEY talks to POPO's swing.

SHIRLEY: It's so hot my socks are sticking to my legs.

(To the swing.) I don't know how you do it. What happens when it's really sunny, do you burn people's bums? I bet you do. I bet you look up people's dresses too, to see what colour knickers they've got on. What colour knickers have I got on?

(In a high pitch voice.) 'Navy'

What d' you say?

(Again the voice.) Navy.

I wish my feet could touch the floor. People say I'm short. I hate that; my teachers, girls at school, the man at the chip shop. Judy, my best friend says all Chinese are short that's why you can't see them behind the takeaway counter. Mum says she's rude and racist. I don't think so, because I don't know what that means.

Pause.

Do you like being green? Do you ever wish you were... another colour?

Must be nice being a swing...sitting around, getting pushed by the wind, listening to people's stories. Except for when it rains, or if it's very sunny, or if people have eaten a lot of food.

If I push my legs hard can you help me touch the sky? Like those geese that fly across the sea? Higher and higher and higher.

She swings, really going for it. The swing is starting to show some strain.

MEI SUN: *(Off.)* Shirley, come and take a bath.

I'm going to count to three... One, two...

SHIRLEY: I don't want a bath.

MEI SUN: *(Off.)* Two and a quarter...

SHIRLEY: There isn't any bath tub.

MEI SUN: *(Off.)* Two and a half..

SHIRLEY: There isn't even a toilet seat. I've had my legs crossed since morning.

(To the swing.) Don't worry. I won't pee my pants. I've got good bladder control. All my teachers say so.

MEI SUN: *(Off.)* Two and four fifths.

SHIRLEY: Mum's good at fractions. She says I spend three quarters of my time staring into space, and half of my life in the bathroom.

Pretends to be her mother.

Shirley what are you doing?

I check to see if my breasts are growing...*(has a quick look)* so far nothing.

She then pretends to check her face in the mirror, takes a deep breath, puts her hands together as if in prayer and begins to mumble an incantation.

Lord of light bestow upon me. Opal blue eyes, bluer than the sea. Bleach my skin, fair and white. Unbraid my hair of black and night.

MEI SUN: Are you ignoring me?

I've been calling and calling.

SHIRLEY: I don't think she likes me.

MEI SUN: Who?

SHIRLEY: The old lady.

MEI SUN: That old lady is your grandmother. Of course she likes you. She loves you.

SHIRLEY: She keeps mumbling. I don't know what she's saying. And she smells funny. Why does she keeps stroking my hair and rubbing my skin like I had dirt on it?

MEI SUN: She can't see properly. She probably thinks you have got dirt.

SHIRLEY: You're lying.

MEI SUN: This isn't England. If you behave badly it reflects on me. Like just now. Why didn't you pay respects to your ancestors?

SHIRLEY: I don't know them. I've never met them before.

MEI SUN: That's why you have to pay respect.

SHIRLEY: I don't know what to say?

MEI SUN: You don't say anything. Just hold the joss sticks and bow three times.

SHIRLEY: Why?

MEI SUN: It doesn't matter why. Just do it.

SHIRLEY: Aren't they squashed?

MEI SUN: What?

SHIRLEY: Up there on the table.

Do you think they can really smell the flowers? Or taste the apples? Will the food taste funny after they've eaten it?

MEI SUN: When we pray to our ancestors, we link arms with them. They're our chain to the past.

SHIRLEY: That can't be right. The dead don't have arms.

MEI SUN sighs and starts to chase SHIRLEY. SHIRLEY runs in the house screaming.

SHIRLEY: Aaaargghhh.

MEI SUN is alone by the swing. She sees a sarong hanging on the swing. She bunches it up to make a sarong baby 'you-na' i.e bouncer. She pulls the hammock up and down as if she is rocking a child to sleep. She sings a lullaby her mother used to sing to her.

MEI SUN: Ah long chee chor

Chok tan chong kor

Ai chee long kok

Poi nee chu choke. *(Repeat 4x)*

She sings the song gently at first, and this is matched by the swinging of the bouncer, but the more she sings it the more violent the motion of the bouncer becomes. At the end she lets go of the sarong. The sarong bounces sharply up, and the pole with all of the clothes on falls to the floor. RONG YIN and AH JUN come out to see what all the noise is.

AH JUN: Aiyoh!

RONG YIN: What happened?

MEI SUN: Sorry. I'll help you put them back.

AH JUN picks up a few of the clothes, and see they are dirty.

AH JUN: Now must wash again.

MEI SUN: Sorry. I don't know...how I... I'm really sorry.

AH JUN: Say sorry so many times for what? Sorry cannot change anything.

RONG YIN: Ah Jun.

AH JUN: It's true.

AH JUN exits with the dirty clothes.

RONG YIN: Sorry.

They both laugh.

Pause.

Ah Jun likes the soap bars very much. She says they remind her of her home town.

Pause.

MEI SUN: Ma, looks old....her hair...

RONG YIN: One day she woke up, looked in the mirror and her hair was all white.

MEI SUN: Does she know?

RONG YIN: I told the doctor not to tell her. But she knows.

You want to see the doctor's report? Maybe you can explain some of the medical terms.

MEI SUN: Maybe later.

Pause.

RONG YIN: Is it strange being home after so many years?

MEI SUN: Not really. The kampong is the same. This angsana tree will be here forever.

RONG YIN: Not for long. Everything is changing. The government has big plans. It wants to clear all the kampongs and build flats. HDB flats.

When you left there was high unemployment, bombs, fires, fighting on the street. But the government is working hard to make things better. In September, for the first time, the Southeast Asian Peninsular Games will be held in Singapore. But Singapore can never be England.

Sometimes during exam period when it's quiet. I take out your letters, and read them, afterwards, I read them again. I imagine your house, your garden, your hospital. It is like I'm there too. I feel happy and mark my papers faster. At least one of us is a success.

MEI SUN: *Ko*, (elder brother) I'm not a success.

RONG YIN: No need to be humble. This whole village only you have been to England. Others can only see from magazines.

Yesterday, the deputy principal asked me for advice. He said he wants to send his children to London to study. But we both know even a deputy principal cannot afford. He can only dream. You are living everyone's dream.

MEI SUN: *Ko...*

RONG YIN: You give Ma face...stop people laughing at her.

MEI SUN: I need to tell you something...

RONG YIN: The other day, that dirty prostitute came to our house.

MEI SUN: She's not a prostitute.

RONG YIN: She's a bar girl. Same thing.

MEI SUN: That's not fair.

RONG YIN: Why are you defending a cheap bar girl?

You know, she had the cheek to ask Ma if she wanted anything.

MEI SUN: What did Ma say?

RONG YIN: She said 'I want to see you swallow atomic bomb.'

You should have seen that prostitute's face...all red and puffy up.

Ah, don't talk about that cheap slut anymore. What did you want to tell me?

MEI SUN: I....it's nothing.

RONG YIN: So your in-laws still live by the sea? *(Before MEI SUN can reply, he starts singing.)* 'Oh I do like to be beside the seaside, oh I do like to be beside the sea... I do like to stroll along the Prom Prom Prom! Where the brass band plays tiddley–om-pom-pom.'

Hahaha. A great British song. I'm so happy your husband comes from a good family.

MEI SUN: My mother-in-law, is very English. She likes to cook a roast – roast beef, roast potatoes, carrots, peas. And for dessert – bread and butter pudding.

RONG YIN: And your job at the hospital, it pays well?

MEI SUN: Yes. I'm very lucky.

Pause.

RONG YIN: Mei Sun...

As your older brother...it is only right I support you.

In a foreign land you have no one. What happens if you're cold? Or hungry? It's only right... When we were courting I said to Ah Jun, 'One day when we're married, I will buy a car. We will dress up nice, drive to Changi, swim in the sea, and eat *lok lok*.' She'd say, 'When Rong Yin? When?' And I'd say, 'When you carry my first born child.'

The baby is coming...but my teacher's pay is so little. We have spent all our savings on Ma's party.

So...not now, but soon, can you give me back the money I gave you...

You have a steady job. Should be no problem, right?

MEI SUN: No problem. No problem at all.

POPO: *(Off stage.)* Rong. Rong. Come quickly. Ah Jun is hurt.

SHIRLEY: *(Off stage.)* She slipped on one of the soaps Mum.

POPO: *(Off stage.)* She is bleeding. Come quickly.

RONG YIN: Ah Jun. Ah Jun.

RONG YIN goes to exit but stops and looks at MEI SUN who sits frozen.

Are you coming?

SCENE 6 – THESE THINGS HAPPEN

MEI SUN walks over to her swing, and starts to move slowly and seductively around it, twisting and turning her body, almost pole dancing. Then she begins to thrust her hips, on one part of the swing and then another, and then another, and then another, if this can be timed with a rhythmic motion of the swing that would be better. This goes on as she speaks. She starts slowly and seductively but end up violent and urgent as she reaches a climax.

MEI SUN: I once watched a gecko slip in the back of my cousin's dress.

She unaware, until she felt the claws pierce her skin.

I once watched a bent willow dip into a brook.

The brook unaware until she felt it quivering in her ripples.

I once watched two twenty pound notes slip into a wallet.

The wallet unaware until she felt its smoothness inside her.

The movements start to become more violent and urgent.

I once watched a sword thrust into the belly of a whale.

The whale unaware until the blood seeped sidewards.

I once watched a grenade pushed into the mouth of a child

The child unaware until she saw patterns on the cement of a country home, red roses blooming, arched doorways, cast-iron gates, lace curtains, soft cushions, linoleum, checked table cloths, wardrobes with pearl handles, quilted blankets, holidays in Majorca, shiny saucepans, chipped teacups, colour TV, silver napkin rings, cucumber sandwiches, chocolate biscuits, roast potatoes, peas, carrots, houses by the sea, the sea, the sea.

I once watched a grenade pushed into the mouth of a child.

END OF ACT ONE.

Act Two

SCENE ONE - SHATTERED DREAMS

POPO's swing is empty. AH JUN wears a dressy cheongsam with her best jewels and a big sun hat. She carries a bag suitable for the beach. She puts the bag down and sits on the edge of the swing as if waiting for someone. She waits and hums then sings the Hakka song – 'Bright Moonlight' (Ngiet gong gong) as in scene 1.

MEI SUN is upstage in front of POPO's swing. She puts on thermal underwear, a jumper, trousers, a big overcoat, scarves, a woolly hat and gloves. She walks over to her swing, sits and waits. The DIRECTOR walks in carrying a clip board. He is caucasian but played by the same actor who plays RONG YIN. He speaks with a strong cockney accent (like Michael Caine).

DIRECTOR: Right then, who's next?

> *He flicks through the papers on his clipboard.*

> Have we got a Meiii SunTan here? Meii SunTan?

> *MEI SUN does not recognise her name and continues to sit.*

> No? Moving on then.

> *Suddenly MEI SUN realises she's been called. She jumps up.*

MEI SUN: It's me. I'm Mei Sun. I'm Mei Sun Tan.

DIRECTOR: So you are... Hello love. I'm Lawrence Wright. I'm the director of this film. If you'd like to follow me. This way please.

> *They move to another space. The director writes on the clipboard.*

Right then, just a bit of admin to get through, then you can show me what you can do. Is that good? Okay?

So, name... Meiii SunTan. Is that right? Am I pronouncing it right?

MEI SUN: *(Pronouncing it properly.)* Actually, it's Mei Sun... Tan.

DIRECTOR: Right. That's what I said Meiii SunTan.

You may want to change that to something simpler, like Mary...or Jane. Mary Tan. Jane Tan. Much easier on the tongue... Shall we do that?

MEI SUN: Sorry? Do what?

DIRECTOR: Change it. Call you Mary...unless your prefer Jane.

MEI SUN: Erm... Mr. Wright I... I prefer it if you can call me... Mei Sun.

DIRECTOR: If that's how you feel. Just trying to help.

So where are you from Meiii...?

MEI SUN: I'm from Singapore.

DIRECTOR: Lovely. That's lovely. And where is that love?

MEI SUN: Ermm... It's near Indonesia.

DIRECTOR: Oh. Indonesia. Right.

And where is that near....

MEI SUN: Ermm... China?

DIRECTOR: China. Got it. Great. Just what we're looking for.

Can you sing?

MEI SUN: Yes I can.

DIRECTOR: Great. Go ahead.

MEI SUN: 'Moon river wider than a...'

DIRECTOR: No...no I mean one of your songs. A Chinese song.

MEI SUN: You mean a Mandarin song?

DIRECTOR: Whatever.

MEI SUN: I can't.

DIRECTOR: What?

MEI SUN: I can't speak Mandarin. I went to a mission school.

The DIRECTOR looks at his watch. He's starting to get bored.

DIRECTOR: Can't you make it up? It's not like I'd know the difference. *(He laughs at his joke.)*

MEI SUN begins to sing the Hakka song – 'Bright Moonlight' (Ngiet gong gong). She sings it with all her heart. The DIRECTOR appears to be spell bound, but halfway he stops her.

DIRECTOR: That was lovely dear, you're a real song bird. But it doesn't sound right. You know what I'm saying? It doesn't...how do I put it...sound Chinese enough... sorry love but you're not really what we're looking for.

MEI SUN: *(Realising she is about to be dismissed, tries to salvage the situation.)* I'm sorry I disappointed you Mr. Wright. Please let me try again. I can do it. I really can. Please let me try.

DIRECTOR: Okay.

MEI SUN tries to sing again in 'made up Mandarin' but it sounds awful.

DIRECTOR: That was bloody awful...you're just not what we're...

MEI SUN: I'm an artist Mr. Wright. I can sing. I can dance. I'm a really good dancer. Please let me dance for you. Please, give me this chance.

MEI SUN hums 'Ngiet gong gong' and begins to dance, she dances with grace and beauty. The DIRECTOR is impressed. He claps.

DIRECTOR: That was very good.

MEI SUN: Thank you.

DIRECTOR: Well done.

MEI SUN: Thank you Mr. Wright.

DIRECTOR: Now love...why don't you try that again, this time without your clothes.

MEI SUN: You want me to take my clothes off?

DIRECTOR: That's right.

MEI SUN: In front of you?

DIRECTOR: You said you were an artist.

You do want to be an actress don't you?

MEI SUN: Ever since I was little girl.

DIRECTOR: Then as an actress you have do what the director says. Or are you saying you can't follow directions?

MEI SUN: No. No... I can... I can...

DIRECTOR: Then what are you waiting for?

Mary, can I call you Mary?

MEI SUN nods.

Do you know what I ate for breakfast this morning?

Nothing. Haven't eaten a thing all morning. And you want to know why? Because I've been too busy listening to girls just like you, come in here with their long hair and high heels, all wanting to be the next Ingrid Bergman or Judy Garland. So I don't need to hear another 'little girl dream' story, because frankly they bore me and I don't give a fuck. We all have dreams but most of us write them on an envelope and shove them under our pillow hoping they'll magically turn into reality. Well I'm here to tell you that's fucking Santa Claus shit. There is no Santa Claus. There is no tooth fairy. There is only those that do, and those that don't.

You lot come to this country expecting something. Let me tell you something. Nobody is going to give you nothing. If you want anything you got to grab it. Grab it by the balls with your teeth and hold on for dear life. I'm telling you straight. I'm telling you for free.

There aren't many roles for persons of your colour. You got to take what comes because you don't know when it'll come again. You do what you need because that is the only way to get anything in this fucking life. Do you understand what I'm saying?

Time almost freezes.

MEI SUN starts to take off all of her clothes one by one. She hums 'Ngiet gong gong', this is echoed by AH JUN.

SCENE 2 – 10 DAYS AFTER END OF ACT ONE

Lights up on POPO's swing. AH JUN sits, waiting. SHIRLEY rushes out. She is playing hide and seek with POPO. She hides in and around the swing.

SHIRLEY: Cover your eyes with your hands and start counting.

Are you counting?

I can't hear you.

POPO: *(Hakka.)* One, two, three...four, five...

SHIRLEY: I'll shout when I'm ready. Then come and get me.

SHIRLEY rushes about the swing trying to find the perfect hiding spot. AH JUN sits motionless on the swing in her own world. Finally SHIRLEY finds a spot.

I'm ready. Come and get me.

Popo... I'm ready...come and get me.

Popo... I'm waiting.

POPO: *(POPO pretends to look for SHIRLEY.)* Eight, nine... Where is she? She must be here. Huh? No...no... Eh?

SHIRLEY giggles and slowly moves around the swing trying to dodge POPO. POPO continues with the farce.

Cannot see her anywhere.

Shirley. Where are you?

Has monster eaten you for dinner?

Suddenly, SHIRLEY screams out from behind POPO. POPO is taken by surprise.

SHIRLEY: Boo!!! Aarghhhhh...

POPO: Aiyoh. Don't scare me like that. Can die from heart attack.

SHIRLEY: Gotchya.

POPO: Okay enough playing. Popo tired. Come.

POPO sits on the swing. She pats the swing to beckon SHIRLEY to join her, but SHIRLEY has taken an interest in AH JUN. She stands in front of her and waves her hand trying to get a response. AH JUN continues to stare out blankly.

SHIRLEY: What is she doing?

Is she going to be alright?

POPO: She is waiting for her dream to come true.

SHIRLEY: Will she have to wait long?

POPO: Very long.

SHIRLEY: There was a girl like that in our school.
She used to stand in the playground, and show us her knickers. But when she pulled her hair out, and put it in our lunch boxes, the teachers got a counsellor in. Will you have to get a counsellor?

Popo have you ever been sad?

You know what I do when I'm sad?

I play pretend. I play pretend a lot... So does mummy.

Pause.

POPO grabs SHIRLEY's hand and pulls her towards the swing.

POPO: Close your eyes.

Can you still see my face?

SHIRLEY nods vigorously.

What do you see?

SHIRLEY: Two eyes a nose and a mouth.

POPO shakes her head. She grabs SHIRLEY's hands and puts them on her face.

POPO: Use your hands to see.

POPO moves SHIRLEY's hands around, over every wrinkle and curve of her face. SHIRLEY is still with her eyes still shut.

Now tell me.

SHIRLEY: I see two mountains. Between them is a valley. And in the valley is a forest of christmas trees. The trees are tall and strong because of water from two ponds. One pond is bigger than the other. On the other side of the trees are two small rivers leading to a big cave. Inside the cave it is dark but sometimes rays of sunlight appear.

POPO: Next time you think of me, I will know.

SHIRLEY: How will you know?

POPO: Last time your grandfather don't want me to follow here. But I want to follow. So, I take all my precious things, and put inside my blue cloth.

Ship got many people. Very crowded. Hot, smelly. Only one toilet. I tell my girl hold tight, if not later cannot find you. Next morning, somebody scream, I see my girl gone. I call her, she never answer, then my heart know what my eyes don't want to see.

Sometimes at night, she play on the swing. Or maybe it's the wind.

POPO takes SHIRLEY's hand and puts it on the arm of the swing.

See here? *(She puts SHIRLEY's fingers on the marks on the swing.)* One, two, three.

When I touch like this, I know she is here.

SHIRLEY: Roooooar.

SHIRLEY jumps up. POPO laughs. MEI SUN enters.

MEI SUN: Shirley no more playing. Go and get ready.

Go on.

I'll be there in a minute.

SHIRLEY touches the three lines on the swing, and exits.

Ma...sorry I can't stay for the party.

POPO: I know.

MEI SUN: Remember to take lots of....photos.

Pause.

Next year you should come to England. We can go to Buckingham Palace together and see the Queen.

POPO: See first.

POPO gets up. MEI SUN suddenly rushes forward and hugs her tightly. POPO allows her to do this, but doesn't respond, she simply pats her on the back.

Go.

POPO goes to AH JUN.

Come Ah Jun. We come back tomorrow.

MEI SUN sits in the same position as AH JUN. RONG YIN enters with a basket of washing. He hangs the clothes. MEI SUN helps.

MEI SUN: Why don't you ask Ma to postpone the party? Until Ah Jun is...

RONG YIN: We have already postponed it for three days. Any longer the food will go bad and all the money wasted.

MEI SUN: I'm going to ask the hospital for a short term loan...it's a higher rate...but...

I'm sorry I wasn't more help – with Ah Jun.

I was tired. Light-headed. Jetlagged.

It could have happened to anyone.

RONG YIN: That's what I told Ma.

Pause.

MEI SUN: I'll get you your money, *Ko*. I don't care how many hours I have to work. I'll get it. I promise. Just give me time.

RONG YIN: The other day Ma asked for your school certificate.

And the photo of you in your nurse uniform.

MEI SUN: Why?

RONG YIN: These are her most treasured possessions.

Nursing is a good profession. You must work hard. Don't let others bully you. One day, maybe you can be a sister or a matron.

MEI SUN: *Ko*... I...

RONG YIN: I have given Shirley durian cake to give to her grandparents. She cannot go home empty handed.

MEI SUN: Thank you.

RONG YIN: I still hope to go to England one day... Big Ben, Buckingham Palace, Stratford-upon-Avon. So much history, so much culture. So much class. The English know how to do things properly.

SHIRLEY enters with her suitcase.

SHIRLEY: Mum my bag smells funny. Smell.

SHIRLEY opens her bag.

MEI SUN: Where is Popo?

SHIRLEY: She said 'one goodbye is enough, words we forget, only the body remembers.' What does that mean mum?

RONG YING: Come give your uncle a hug. Who knows when we'll again? Maybe next time we meet you will have your own children.

SHIRLEY: I don't think so. I'm not even married yet.

RONG YIN: Study hard and you will be successful, and make us all proud.

MEI SUN: Bye *Ko*. Take care of Ma and Ah Jun.

MEI SUN and SHIRLEY exit. They weave in and out of the swings and arrive at MEI SUN's swing. MEI SUN looks to POPO's swing one more time.

SHIRLEY: Will I ever see Popo again?

MEI SUN: I don't know sweetheart.

SHIRLEY: I do. Popo showed me how. She told me to see with my hands. Like this. *(She demonstrates.)* Then I can see her anytime I want.

Mum... I love Popo.

I love Popo more than Nana.

MEI SUN: *(She takes SHIRLEY's hands and holds them tight.)* Watch the lady do her demonstration. It might save your life.

SCENE 3 – POPO'S JOURNEY

POPO is curled up on the swing. She writhes in pain, but slowly as the swing moves, she is lulled to sleep.

When the swing stops. POPO lays motionless. RONG YIN comes in and carries POPO away. The stage is empty except for the still swing.

SCENE 4 – AH JUN IS HOME LATE – 1976

RONG YIN sits on the swing for AH JUN's return. AH JUN returns, tipsy. The following altercation takes places around the swing. Preferably choreographed.

RONG YIN: You said eight thirty. It's nearly eleven.

AH JUN: Forgot the time.

RONG YIN: Where have you been?

AH JUN: They won all 69 seats. PAP. PAP.

RONG YIN: Since when you so interested in politics.

    You smell of alcohol and cigarettes.

    I want you to stop working in the shop.

    I want you to stay at home.

AH JUN: And do what? Sit on the swing all day like your mother?

RONG YIN: People are laughing at me.

    The deputy principal told me his wife saw you.

AH JUN: She wanted brown but they didn't have her size.

RONG YIN: You touched her feet?

AH JUN: It's my job.

RONG YIN: Ah Jun. You have to stop. I'm the laughing stock of the staff room. An English teacher's wife selling shoes.

AH JUN: What's so big about being your wife?

    An English teacher who never even been to England.

RONG YIN: I have a reputation.

    With the principal, my colleagues, my student's parents.

AH JUN: You forgotten? Government build flats, but flat not free. We need money.

RONG YIN: Ah Mei will send the money.

AH JUN: Ah Mei?

Three years already. Still the money never come. Only letters about her garden, what her girl eat for breakfast. Who cares? Where is our money?

RONG YIN: She said...

AH JUN: She said. She said. Only you believe. She says she is a nurse still you believe her.

What kind of nurse faint when she sees blood?

RONG YIN: Don't say any more.

AH JUN: If she is real nurse she can help me...then maybe...today I can still have children.

RONG YIN: I said enough. No more.

AH JUN: Who knows how many lies we swallow?

My belly is full of her lies.

RONG YIN: Ah Jun.

AH JUN: Until I want to vomit. And her girl...

RONG YIN: Don't Ah Jun...

AH JUN: Who is her father? A doctor? How come we never see him? No photo. Not even one lousy picture.

RONG YIN: He died after she was born. You know that.

AH JUN: How convenient. Then where the photos of his parents? Where the photo of the house by to the sea? More lies.

She is probably a bastard. Your niece is a bastard. The English teacher's niece is a bastard.

At that RONG YIN goes to slap AH JUN, but he stops himself. AH JUN almost hysterical.

Go ahead do it. Do it. Do it. You know long words but you don't know how to be a man.

RONG YIN pushes the swing and exits. AH JUN collapses from the emotion. Then resumes the 'waiting' position on the swing from earlier.

SCENE 5 – PAVED WITH GOLD

RONG YIN moves to another space and begins to dress up in winter clothes.

AH JUN is still sitting at the swing waiting. MEI SUN is at her swing.

RONG YIN: Dear Mei Sun

MEI SUN: Dear *Ko*

RONG YIN: I want

MEI SUN: I want

RONG YIN: To tell you I'm coming to England.

MEI SUN: To thank you for the photo of Ma's tree. I'm sure she'll be very happy there.

RONG YIN: But I want to surprise you.

MEI SUN: It's the perfect place for her ashes.

RONG YIN: To see the look on your face.

MEI SUN: The weather is warm and many fruits are in season; oranges, apples, raspberries and pears,

RONG YIN: I want to see your beautiful rose garden.

MEI SUN: Shirley has developed a taste for coffee.

RONG YIN: The flight was smooth.

MEI SUN: She is doing well in school.

RONG YIN: I had no problem with immigration.

MEI SUN: Last week she was top for Mathematics and Science.

RONG YIN: Customs searched my luggage very thoroughly.

MEI SUN: The teacher gave her two gold stars.

RONG YIN: When I reached your road, I thought there was a mistake.

MEI SUN: She seldom makes mistakes. Her spelling is excellent.

RONG YIN: I asked the taxi driver if the address was correct.

MEI SUN: She studies hard because she wants to be successful.

RONG YIN: There is no cul-de sac or rose garden.

MEI SUN: And earn lots of money so we can travel the world together.

RONG YIN: Only cracked windows covered with wooden planks.

MEI SUN stops talking and just looks at RONG YIN as if she has just realised what he is saying. They stare at one another.

And I see you. You hold Shirley's hand. I call you but you don't hear me. I follow you to school. Some schoolboys call you 'chink'. They throw stones. You say nothing. You put your head down and carry on walking.

MEI SUN: *(Speaking honestly.)* After I send Shirley to school, I go home and do the washing. On Friday, I vacuum the carpet. I take the number 70 bus –

RONG YIN: And go to Chinatown. Where is your uniform?

MEI SUN: Even when it's sunny, the Zebraman club is always dark. The customers like it that way.

RONG YIN: I watch you enter.

MEI SUN: The music is always the same, but nobody cares because nobody listens.

RONG YIN: You know this place. You have been here many times.

MEI SUN: I share a dressing room with eight other girls.

RONG YIN: I ask the barman if he knows you. He doesn't.

MEI SUN: I do the day shift. Shirley doesn't like to be alone at night.

RONG YIN: And I see you.

MEI SUN: And I see you.

RONG YIN: Standing still.

MEI SUN: Barely breathing. Unable to move.

RONG YIN: Until someone shouts.

MEI SUN: Until someone shouts.

RONG YIN: 'Come on Mary.'

MEI SUN: 'Come on Mary.'

RONG YIN: 'Get 'em knickers off.'

MEI SUN: 'Get 'em off', 'Get 'em off', 'Get 'em off.'

And I do.

RONG YIN: I cannot watch.

MEI SUN: I'm an artist. I'm a dancer.

RONG YIN: I cannot watch.

MEI SUN: I dance very well.

RONG YIN: Watch you straddle your legs on their laps.

MEI SUN: I make good tips.

RONG YIN: Watch your tongue on their lips.

MEI SUN: But some men want more.

RONG YIN: And I ask.

MEI SUN: You ask.

RONG YIN: *(Points.)* Is he Shirley's father?

MEI SUN: No.

RONG YIN: *(Points.)* Is he Shirley's father?

MEI SUN: No.

RONG YIN: Who is Shirley's father?

RONG YIN/MEI SUN: *(Shouts.)* They're all Shirley's father.

   Pause.

MEI SUN: You turn and run. Face hidden beneath your collar.

RONG YIN: Chest gripped into a fist.

MEI SUN: Legs shorter than I remember.

RONG YIN: In the sunlight I shout.

MEI SUN: In the sunlight no one hears you.

   I feel Ma's blessings every day.

RONG YIN: I have failed Ma.

MEI SUN: I feel Ma's blessings every day.

RONG YIN: I have failed Pa.

   I have failed Ah Jun.

MEI SUN: Ma, can see everything now.

RONG YIN: And I have failed you Ah Mei.

   RONG YIN exits. AH JUN enters with a pot of black paint and begins to paint the swing black.

MEI SUN: Ma has mountains to climb and rivers to swim. When she is tired she rests under shaded trees, and eats ripe peaches before they fall. And when the wind stops howling and stars no longer light the sky she will hear my heart and know why dreams change.

   Please find enclosed the money that I owe you.

   Your devoted sister,

   Mei Sun.

   AH JUN continues to paint the swing black.

SCENE 6– DANCE OF LIFE

RONG YIN pulls MEI SUN to POPO's swing. They dance around as children, but the dance changes and ends with them separated.

A dance:

Of chasing, of laughter.

Falling into one another

Falling away from one another

Falling down and getting up

Circling one another.

Of pushing and pulling

Of high and low.

Of separation

Of separation

Of backs turned.

AH JUN has finished painting the swing. She pulls RONG YIN away and sits him down on the swing gently. He takes up the 'waiting' position. SHIRLEY takes MEI SUN's hand and brings her towards the tree.

SCENE 7 – PRAYER FOR THE DEAD

In front of the tree, SHIRLEY places a packet of chocolate digestives, Kit Kats and a packet of lemon sherbets. She looks at the tree reverently.

MEI SUN: What are you doing?

Solemnly SHIRLEY takes three slow bows.

SHIRLEY: Shush. I'm paying my respects to Popo and the others. I don't know their names.

SHIRLEY takes out three straws from her pockets and sticks them in the ground near the tree.

MEI SUN: With three straws, chocolate digestives and lemon sherbets?

SHIRLEY: And a packet of Kit Kats.

MEI SUN: But why?

SHIRLEY: Because I don't have enough space.

Yesterday I learnt long division, and that Henry the eighth had six wives. Tomorrow we're going to learn about stalagmites and stalactites. I try to remember like Popo taught me...between two mountains there is a valley and in the valley there is...there is...but I don't have enough space. New things push out the old. And if I can't see Popo's face, she won't know I'm thinking of her. Will she?

MEI SUN: Come here.

MEI SUN takes SHIRLEY's hand and together they bow and then kneel by the tree in front of the 'altar'.

SHIRLEY: I don't know what to say.

MEI SUN: Say what's in your heart.

When the wind blows, the leaves will carry your words to Popo.

SHIRLEY: You say something too.

MEI SUN: I don't know what to say.

MEI SUN looks at SHIRLEY and smiles. They begin their incantations. As they say them POPO enters and sits on her swing.

SHIRLEY: I love Popo and she loves me.

MEI SUN: A life unpeeled reveals another.

SHIRLEY: I love Popo and she loves me.

MEI SUN: A life unpeeled reveals another.

SHIRLEY: I love Popo and she loves me.

RONG YIN still sitting on POPO's swing takes out money from his pocket and throws it into the air. MEI SUN and SHIRLEY look up and see the money fluttering in the wind, like leaves.

SCENE 8 – THESE ARE A FEW OF MY FAVOURITE THINGS

All three women are swinging on their swings.

MEI SUN: A hot bacon roll with lots of HP sauce.

SHIRLEY: Silk tassels unravelling in the wind.

AH JUN: Dried chillies sitting in the sun.

MEI SUN: Microwave dinners and Big Brother on repeat.

SHIRLEY: Tracing icicles on a window pane.

AH JUN: Drinking beer in coffee shops.

MEI SUN: Carol singing outside Tescos.

SHIRLEY: Kitchen drawers closing silently.

AH JUN: Playing one-armed bandit...and winning.

    Pause.

MEI SUN: I don't remember.

SHIRLEY: Starlit waterfalls in a forest of pine.

AH JUN: The wind drying my sarong on the washing line.

SHIRLEY: *(To MEI SUN.)* Shifting marble slabs in open seas.

MEI SUN: Sorry, I still don't remember.

SCENE 9 – POPO'S ASHES

AH JUN: Dearest Shirley, I write to tell you – your uncle Rong Yin has passed away. He has been sick for long time, not in body but in heart. No need to be sad. He is finally at peace, with your Popo. He is happy.

After we divorce we never talk for many years. But before he die, he ask my forgiveness, and tell me everything he has he give to me. Except for your Popo's swing. This one he say must go to you – his niece. He is a funny man. Even I live with him so many years, I still never understand him.

Anyway, I enclose the swing for you.

Kind regards,

Aunty Jun.

SHIRLEY: *(On handphone.)* Hello… Mum? It's me Shirley. Good. Thanks. How are you?

Why didn't you tell me you'd moved?

Right you did. Sorry, I forgot. Been so busy. Work is crazy. No. Everything is fine. I'm settling in great… I'm learning mandarin…and…Mum I've got some bad news about Uncle Rong Yin…he… Who told you? Yes it just got here. I put it in my dining/living room. No…it's fine. I…have plenty of space.

Listen, Mum, I know you have your life and I have mine. I don't want to assume anything. But… I was wondering, why don't you come to Shanghai? You've never been to China. I could send you a ticket…we could go to that village in Guangzhou…to the tree… where Popo's ashes are scattered.

Pause.

Mum…there are two mountains and between them is a valley. And in the valley is a forest of christmas trees.

The trees are tall and strong because of water from two ponds. One pond is bigger than the other. On the other side of the trees are two small rivers leading to a big cave. Inside the cave it is dark but sometimes... rays of sunlight appear.

SCENE 10 – FINAL SCENE

Lights up on AH JUN, she is old and moves with difficulty. In her hand she holds a big piece of blue cloth. She takes the cloth and slowly wraps POPO's swing with the cloth. She begins to sing the Hakka song (Ngiet gong gong).

Lights up on MEI SUN's swing, she is also old and frail. Her clothes have changed. She has a suitcase by her side. She sits waiting. She begins to sing Ngiet gong gong too, shakily at first. But the more she sings the more confident it becomes. She sings in unison with AH JUN.

THE END.

Before becoming a playwright, **Tan Suet Lee** practiced as a chartered accountant. Since making the switch, she has written a number of plays including: *The Swing* (2017, 2013), *Weight of Emptiness* (2016), *Assassins* (2016), *A Second Life* (2015), *Lies in Waiting* (2011), *Sperm* (2008), *Beautiful Companion* (2006), and *Shopping with Ang* (2004) by Yellow Earth Theatre at the Typhoon 3: International East Asian Playreading Festival. With the support of the Singapore National Arts Council, Suet Lee attended the La MaMa International Playwright Retreat in Umbria, Italy in August 2013 where she developed *The Swing*.

Suet Lee also writes TV and film scripts, short stories and poetry, and was recently awarded third prize for English Poetry at the Golden Point Award, a premier creative writing competition in Singapore. Suet Lee holds an MA in Creative Writing from Swansea University and is currently studying for a PhD in Creative Writing.

I'M JUST HERE TO BUY SOY SAUCE

by JINGAN YOUNG

Production history

I'm Just Here to Buy Soy Sauce was first performed as a work-in-progress at the Camden People's Theatre on the 17th January 2016 as part of their Whose London? festival. It was then extensively developed with Papergang Theatre Company and toured London from May - June 2016 with performances at the New Wimbledon Studio, Old Red Lion Theatre, Islington and the China Exchange, Soho with the following cast and creative team:

Cast

Joyce Veheary

Alex Wilson

Creative

Writer	Jingan Young
Director	Freyja Winterson
Producer	Clarissa Widya, Papergang Theatre
Sound/Lighting Designer	Archie Macleod

It was also revived for a special performance, directed by Rikki Beadle-Blair, at Slam King's Cross from the 17th – 18th June 2017.

The play's development has been supported by Old Vic New Voices, Arcola Theatre's BAMER Lab and the China Exchange's Cultivate Programme.

Dedicated to my mother Kerrie

CONTEXT

By 2025 China will have invested £105+ billion in British infrastructure, primarily in energy, transport and property (*Financial Times*, October 27 2014). In October 2013 Chancellor George Osborne relaxed UK visa rules making it possible for any number of Chinese citizens to visit (and invest in) the UK. In 2014 Chinese nationals were granted the most Tier 1 visas, which fast tracks the immigration process for those who want to invest more than £1m.

In 2012 Chinese wealth fund China Investment Corporation bought a 10% stake in Thames Water. Iconic London black cabs were saved from bankruptcy by Chinese firm Geely. In December 2015, China Media Capital invested £300m (13% stake) in Manchester City FC.

A £1bn redevelopment of London's Docklands by a Chinese investment firm will turn the area into the UK's 'third biggest financial district'. Mayor of London Boris Johnson was quoted as being 'thrilled', offering his full endorsement for the scheme.

In 2013 there were an estimated 50,000 empty homes in the nation's capital. That number continues to rise.

Characters

CASSANDRA WU

CHARMAINE MOK

FREDDIE REYNOLDS

FRASER HAMILTON

Generally dialogue is spoken very quickly but concisely. Characters hide behind words; their preferred weapon of choice.

(/) indicates the next speech begins from that point.

(-) indicates the next line interrupts.

(...) means the speech trails off signalling the character is in hesitation or expectation.

A line with no full stop indicates the next speech begins immediately.

Staging

Although different characters, they may be played by the same actors. In terms of staging - minimal. However there could be a 'model home/doll house' that can be easily manipulated, placed somewhere on stage. There should be a large screen placed upstage. Transitions are swift.

SCENE ONE

Offices/Marketing Suite of Avarita International Global Worldwide Properties Ltd., inside a newly built skyscraper. Far East London. Panoramic views.

CASSANDRA (suited) is sat cross-legged on the floor. She appears to be meditating. Her shoes and mobile are by her ankles. Perhaps she's holding a copy of Sun Tzu's 'The Art of War'. FREDDIE enters sweaty, breathless...

FREDDIE: *Sosorryliftsbroken*

> *Beat.*

> *(Breathless.)* Felt like my lungs were about to protrude through my muscles, veins, cavities...

> *CASSANDRA remains fixed on the floor.*

> What a view! 'Spiritus Mundi'! You can even see the river *and* that Olympic monstrosity...

> *He trails off. Awkward.*

> Know what my dad calls it? He calls it the 'crack pipe piece of crap'. He's got a point though. I mean, who on *earth* would think something like *that* was a good idea for the London skyline?

> *He remembers himself.*

> Honestly! My mind has this tendency to fly away. Almost as if the idea ascends, is burned by the sun and then – dust. Like in that Greek myth, *Icarus*? Gotta love the metaphor. Corruptibility of fame, false ambition. Sorry! Here I am blah blah blah-ing away. You must think I'm some psychopath waltzing in here unannounced going on about crack pipes.

> *He puts out his hand.*

> Freddie Reynolds. Apologies. Overground –

CASSANDRA: Do you know what the Chinese have baptised Anish Kapoor's self-proclaimed 'masterpiece'?

FREDDIE: As a matter of fact –

CASSANDRA: 'Zhai Xing Ta'.

FREDDIE: Actually, it's –

CASSANDRA: 'The tower that allows us to pluck the majestic stars from the sky.'

FREDDIE: Ring to it.

CASSANDRA: 'Appear weak when you are strong, strong when you are weak.'

FREDDIE: Sorry?

CASSANDRA: 'He who wins knows when to fight and when *not* to fight.'

FREDDIE: I don't understand!

CASSANDRA: 'He who wins, knows how to handle both superior *and* inferior forces.'

FREDDIE: I have an interview?

CASSANDRA: 'I will not interrupt my superior whilst she is detached from all-worldly pleasures.'

FREDDIE: Oh! Sun Tzu's *The Art of War.*

Beat.

CASSANDRA: 'All warfare is based on deception.'

FREDDIE: *(Joking, though not really...)* 'Confucius say'?!

CASSANDRA: *Don't* be a fucking racist.

FREDDIE: I wasn't being racist!

CASSANDRA: Shall we get started?

FREDDIE rummages through his bag, finds his CV.

FREDDIE: CV. *(Beat.)* Curriculum. *(Beat.)* Vitae?

He hands it to her. She grunts.

CASSANDRA: Dare to dream Mr. Reynolds.

She discards the CV.

FREDDIE: Who would believe *this (beat, coughs)* bit of this city, which no one even wants to build a Tesco Express on, is on the market for one point five billion pounds.

CASSANDRA: The Chinese!

FREDDIE: Oh but of course. The Chinese.

CASSANDRA: Entrepreneurial wizards, peddlers, pushers, pullers of stock markets, manipulators of algorithms, philanderers, money-launderers... The Chinese!

FREDDIE: Right.

CASSANDRA: And before you ask *why* when there are over 50,000 empty homes across London they would bother buying such a vagrant plot of wasteland. Well –

FREDDIE: The Chinese are superstitious!

CASSANDRA: Bit of a stereotype.

FREDDIE: No. 'Gui Wu'.

CASSANDRA: *What* did you just call me?

He lowers himself to her level.

FREDDIE: Nothing! 'Gui Wu', translates to 'Ghost House'. If something's used, or if someone's died, been murdered in it, the thing, flat, house, home it's automatically designated cursed.

CASSANDRA: Let me guess, you studied Putonghua at University College Nowhere?

He points to his CV.

FREDDIE: Oxford.

CASSANDRA: Oxford?

FREDDIE: Oxford University.

CASSANDRA: College?

FREDDIE: Look Miss, I really don't see how this –

CASSANDRA: It's Cassandra.

FREDDIE: OK.

CASSANDRA: And I despise being called Sisi.

FREDDIE: OK Cassandra.

CASSANDRA: Only my father calls me Sisi...

FREDDIE: This *is* the interview for the Junior Associate position?

CASSANDRA: Should never assume Ducks.

FREDDIE: Which as far as I am aware does not involve being bullied.

CASSANDRA: Previous convictions?

FREDDIE: No.

CASSANDRA: Mortgage?

FREDDIE: No!

CASSANDRA: Kids?

FREDDIE: I'm twenty-six.

CASSANDRA: OK. Your thoughts on the Chinese buying up all of London?

FREDDIE: I've never really thought about it!

CASSANDRA: Ever since Xi Jinping. Oh, you know who that is right? Google it later. Since his 'crackdown' on dirty back-handed business in China those poor lads need somewhere to discharge their surplus.

FREDDIE: Wow.

CASSANDRA: Handing out discounted Tier 1 visas to entrepreneurs from a country with one of the most questionable human rights records to date so they can invest a billion or two benefits everybody Fred.

FREDDIE: How does leaving a block of flats empty 'benefit everybody'?

CASSANDRA: *That* is why you are not right for this job. Your refusal to see the 'Bigger Picture'. Plus you've got like, zero people skills.

FREDDIE: Bigger picture.

CASSANDRA: The Chinese are investing in our crumbling infrastructure

FREDDIE: Actually the Chinese don't see our infrastructure as having any 'real value for money'.

CASSANDRA: Where'd you come up with that stat Ox-bored?

FREDDIE: I *read*.

CASSANDRA: Our government certainly doesn't want to bother with building more homes or buying more trains 'for the people'. Pray tell, what is our alternative, 'the taxpayer'?

FREDDIE: Could I ask you a question?

CASSANDRA: Go right ahead Ducks.

FREDDIE: What do you think of this city?

CASSANDRA: I love London.

FREDDIE: What do you think of the Chinese?

CASSANDRA: I *love* the Chinese. Drawn out negotiations, mind games, pragmatism, unrelenting desire for more, more, more

FREDDIE: You're quite a thing to behold Miss Wu.

CASSANDRA: Cassandra. Please. Oh come now. Don't make that face. Look. Just for fun. Why don't you run along to the corner shop and buy me some champagne?

FREDDIE: Champagne.

CASSANDRA: Chilled.

FREDDIE: I don't have any cash.

She retrieves cash from her handbag.

CASSANDRA: Moet. Dom. Tattinger. *No* cava, and if you buy prosecco...

He takes the cash, exits.

She takes his CV, rips it in half...

'Hold bait to entice the enemy. Feign disorder, crush him'!

She begins laughing.

Suddenly – FREDDIE re-enters, he claps his hands together almost in awe of her viciousness.

FREDDIE: Great! Just great!

CASSANDRA: I'm sorry?

FREDDIE: Congratulations Miss Wu.

CASSANDRA: Wait. You're –

FREDDIE: That's right. I am offering you the Junior Sales and Management position with us here at Avarita.

CASSANDRA: You're fucking with me.

He laughs, shakes his head.

I got the job?

FREDDIE: That whole spiel, 'mind games, pragmatism, unrelenting desire for more'! Where'd you come up with that?

CASSANDRA: Improvised.

FREDDIE: Brilliant!

CASSANDRA: Thank you very much.

FREDDIE: Difficult to pinpoint the precise attributes I was looking for in an assistant. My first time hire you know. But as it turns out – I've got an eye for perfection.

CASSANDRA: You...

FREDDIE: Of course! Proper introductions. Freddie Reynolds. Avarita's Senior Sales and Exhibition Manager. Asian accounts.

He reaches out for her hand, places it in his.

'When you know the enemy and know yourself, you need not fear the battle'. Your performance. Fucking golden.

He chuckles.

CASSANDRA: You can never go wrong with Sun Tzu.

FREDDIE: Make no mistake. This job is no cakewalk. There will be days. *(Beat.)* There will be days. And you still need to meet the partners before we can move forward on this...titillating journey together. Necessary formality I'm afraid.

CASSANDRA: I understand. Like an evaluation?

FREDDIE: Sure. Evaluating your 'skills', level of tolerance, belief in institutions. That sort of thing. That won't be a problem?

She shakes her head.

CASSANDRA: I'm ready for anything.

FREDDIE: Well then. Bold and brazen Cassandra Wu. Welcome to the team.

They shake.

BLACKOUT.

Transition to...

SCENE TWO

Bedroom in a four tenant flatshare. South South South South London.

Lights up on CHARMAINE who is wearing what appears to be fifty layers of clothing. There are packing boxes strewn about the room. Music blares from a laptop (somewhere).

She's attempting to construct a box but is failing. She gives out a cry of irritation.

Suddenly the lights go out.

CHARMAINE: *COME ON!*

> *Door opens. FRASER enters carrying a shopping bag. CHARMAINE trips over a box.*
>
> *Fuck.*

FRASER: Shar?

CHARMAINE: *Fucksake.*

FRASER: Charmaine, *why* are you sitting in the dark?

CHARMAINE: You think I'd voluntarily *choose* to live in a permanent state of semi-blindness?

FRASER: You have been known to 'wallow'.

CHARMAINE: *Don't –*

FRASER: So...

CHARMAINE: No!

FRASER: *You* forgot.

CHARMAINE: No!

> *Lights go back on. CHARMAINE is on the floor surrounded by stuff.*

I did *not* forget to pay the meter. It was Andy. Wanker went on tour.

FRASER: Andy is curled up in the fetal position in a corner by the kitchen.

CHARMAINE: Fuck.

FRASER: *(Laughs.)* Nothing ever changes, eh?

Beat.

CHARMAINE looks at him.

I was in the neighbourhood.

Beat.

Thought I'd spend my Nectar points.

CHARMAINE: Should've let me know Fraser.

FRASER: Let you know that I'd be spending my Nectar points?

CHARMAINE: Bit of a surprise!

FRASER: 'Surprise'! Yes, I should've called first but you would've just said 'no'.

CHARMAINE: I would've said 'fuck off'!

FRASER: But now that I'm here?

CHARMAINE: Here to gloat.

FRASER: To say *hello.*

CHARMAINE: You can't function on 'just a hello'!

FRASER: Loving the new look by the way.

CHARMAINE: Landlord has yet to fix the boiler.

FRASER: But of course!

CHARMAINE: *Here* we go. Please / Stop.

FRASER: Remember when we went for three months without hot water?

CHARMAINE: Not your problem anymore Fraser.

FRASER: Countless times he's pissed off the council...

CHARMAINE: I don't have time for this! *Argh.*

She examines her leg.

FRASER: Charging us for the privilege of living in his –

CHARMAINE: IT'S NOT YOUR BLOODY PROBLEM ANYMORE FRASER ALRIGHT? YOU DON'T LIVE HERE ANYMORE.

Pause.

Sorry.

FRASER: You OK?

CHARMAINE: Only a bruise. Albeit to both left shin *and* ego.

FRASER: I've got steak!

CHARMAINE: You've got what now?

FRASER takes out a package of frozen steak and kidney pies.

FRASER: 600 grams. Sainsbury's finest. Frozen Steak and Kidney Pie.

Beat.

May I?

She nods, he goes over to her, places it delicately on her leg.

Swelling should go down in a couple hours. If not, then I'm the fool who believes 'pie' is the solution to all of mankind's problems.

His hand stays there for a bit too long. She lets it stay there too. After a moment he takes it off.

CHARMAINE: Do you want –

FRASER: Keep it.

CHARMAINE: Thanks.

FRASER: Can I do anything?

CHARMAINE: Go *(beat)* away.

FRASER: 'You can't always get what you want'!

CHARMAINE: Surely you can summon the courage to walk through an estate with one of the worst rates of knife crime, hop on a bus to King's Cross before purchasing an off-peak ticket back to the 'old country', back to your parents

FRASER: Not moving back home

CHARMAINE: Sponging off one of your other upper-middle-class relatives then?

FRASER: Oh-so-mature

CHARMAINE: Simply peachy seeing you Fraser, bye now!

FRASER: Waving the white flag

CHARMAINE: *Please* go away.

FRASER: Sorry about your job.

CHARMAINE: Who told you?

FRASER: Your mum.

CHARMAINE: *Bitch.*

FRASER: She cares.

CHARMAINE: So I was made redundant! Happens everyday. We're the most fucked generation. You know what they're calling freelancing these days? 'Slashing'. Slashing. Slashing! Sometimes I think, only a matter of time

FRASER: Before?

CHARMAINE: 'Everlasting had not fix'd his canon 'gainst self-slaughter'!

FRASER: If you've begun quoting Shakespeare...

CHARMAINE: I am *not* having a nervous breakdown.

FRASER notices the boxes.

Involuntary response. Because that's all you can do really, with an upper second class degree in Comparative Literature.

FRASER: Going on holiday?

CHARMAINE: When did you speak to Mother Mok *anyway*?

FRASER: You're moving?

CHARMAINE: Did she fatten you up with Nasi Goreng in exchange for gossip.

FRASER: You didn't answer my question Shar.

She shrugs.

(Rising.) Where are you going Charmaine?

CHARMAINE: *None* of your business!

FRASER: I don't remember making a 'none of your business' ex-relationship clause!

CHARMAINE: We're *not* mates

FRASER: How can you be so, so...

CHARMAINE: *(Teasing.)* So so so so?

FRASER: *We were going to buy a bloody house together!*

CHARMAINE: I *know* we were going to 'buy a bloody house together'! Thank god we didn't put down a deposit on that pathetic hovel because otherwise we'd be stuck there, for all eternity with absolutely *nothing* to say to one another, having the same argument over and over until we tore one another's flesh off the bone and...

FRASER: You can't think of a better analogy can you?

CHARMAINE: No. Alright? No!

FRASER peeks into a box, pulls out a catalogue.

You didn't *have* to move out. But when the 'going gets tough'...

He reads from the catalogue.

FRASER: 'The most desirable borough in the capital for first-time buyers.'

CHARMAINE: Is that the place we viewed out East?

FRASER: Place you 'loved' the most.

CHARMAINE: I don't know about that.

FRASER: Agent laughed at us for getting there *that* early.

CHARMAINE: Agent was a prick.

FRASER: She was pretty hot.

CHARMAINE: Bloody guffawed after we gave our age. She just couldn't fathom this twenty-something-year-old couple could afford to buy a three hundred and eighty grand one bed flat in a new development.

FRASER: It had a balcony.

CHARMAINE: Black eyes.

FRASER: Black eyes?

CHARMAINE: The agent. She had these piercing black eyes. Cut right through you.

FRASER: Saw right through you anyway.

CHARMAINE: No handshake, no small talk.

FRASER: I remember. Hot pink lips part to reveal sparkling fangs. 'Sorry', she purrs, then shoos us the fuck out. We buy a couple beers, sit by the canal and...

CHARMAINE: You write a bloody poem.

CHARMAINE stands, goes to a box, rifles through it, takes out a notebook, opens it, retrieves a receipt with writing on it. She hands it to him.

FRASER: 'Icarus in Stratford'.

CHARMAINE: Scrawled on a receipt for those Kate Bush records you never listen to...

FRASER: Self-preservation mate.

CHARMAINE: Would you read it to me?

FRASER: I'd rather not.

Pause.

CHARMAINE: You look different.

FRASER: I *am* different.

CHARMAINE: Thinner. Fitter. Or something.

FRASER: I vape now.

CHARMAINE: Good for you.

FRASER: Thanks.

CHARMAINE: *Why* did you come back Fraser?

FRASER: I wanted to tell you, no, to ask you whether you'd consider...

Lights in the room go out.

CHARMAINE: COME ON!

FRASER laughs.

(Unseen.) FUCKSAKE.

FRASER: *(Unseen.)* Now, now. No need for that.

CHARMAINE: *(Unseen.)* Everything's always the big fucking joke with you!

FRASER: *(Unseen.)* Not everything.

CHARMAINE: *(Unseen.)* Stop –

FRASER: *(Unseen.)* God help me I've tried. I love you Shar. I still love you.

CHARMAINE: *(Unseen.)* Stop trying so bloody hard!

FRASER: *(Unseen.)* Impossible!

CHARMAINE: *(Unseen.)* *You* are impossible!

FRASER: *(Unseen.)* I laugh in the face of impossible. Ha, ha, ha, ha!

CHARMAINE: *(Unseen.)* Child.

FRASER: *(Unseen.)* Cynic.

CHARMAINE: *(Unseen.)* Do not push me Fraser.

FRASER: *(Unseen.)* I dare you.

CHARMAINE kisses FRASER.

Lights go back on.

They pull apart.

Well, hello there.

CHARMAINE: Sorry. Habit.

FRASER: Old habits die hard.

FRASER kisses CHARMAINE. They begin tearing one another's clothes off...

BLACKOUT.

Transition to...

SCENE THREE

Training day. Avarita HQ. Far East London.

Spotlight on CASSANDRA seated on a chair centre stage. There is a glass of water by her heels. She appears nervous.

FREDDIE speaks unseen to us and her (for now).

If possible, clips are projected on a screen chronicling the housing crisis intercut with reports detailing China's horrific treatment of pro-democracy activists. This would assist in highlighting the torturous and absurd nature of this training session.

FREDDIE: *(Unseen.)* Now Sisi. Oh! I'm sorry. *Cassandra.* I know you don't like being called Sisi.

CASSANDRA: Absolutely fine Fred.

FREDDIE: *(Unseen.)* Remember Sisi, this is simply a formality. There's nothing to worry about and it will in no way affect the offer of your employment here.

CASSANDRA: Fine. Great.

FREDDIE: *(Unseen.)* If anything, it's more of a 'getting to know you' session. OK?

CASSANDRA: OK

FREDDIE: *(Unseen.)* Ready to wow the rest of the team like you wow'd me in the interview?

CASSANDRA: Ready when you are!

We hear static.

FREDDIE: *(Unseen.)* Excellent. We'll start off with a straightforward roleplay exercise. *Nothing to worry about.* I will play one half of a mid-twenty to thirty something-ish couple looking for a two bed flat and/ or split-level maisonette to suit my socio-economic status and idealistic dreams of parenthood. I've seen an advertisement for a viewing in the *Standard* so I decide to hop on the tube from my humdrum bedsit in Walthamstow to the reflective, gorgeous fifty floors of 'Western Gateway Two'. Got all that?

CASSANDRA: Yep.

FREDDIE: *(Unseen.)* I'm sorry, I didn't quite hear you Sisi.

CASSANDRA: Gotcha!

FREDDIE: *(Unseen.)* Oh and please feel free to make full use of the space Sisi! Flex those sophisticated, speculative, cerebral muscles of yours. We want to see how you *work.*

CASSANDRA: Right.

She stands.

FREDDIE: *(Unseen.)* Shall we begin?

CASSANDRA: Let's do it!

Projection: a selfie of a 'trendy' young woman holding a poodle with a diamanté collar. Think 'Made in Chelsea'.

FREDDIE: *(Unseen.)* Hiya! I'm Binky. I'm twenty-nine. I work in PR. I am looking for a one bed flat for myself and my boyfriend. He's an investment banker in the City but his recent investment in African dictatorships means he's going to follow his dreams of being a DJ. We've been together six months.

Pause.

CASSANDRA: Hello Binky, and terrific. That's terrific. Could I firstly ask whether you are both looking to rent or buy?

FREDDIE: *(Unseen.)* We favour green tea over earl grey. We subscribe to the *Guardian* but we're naughty with *The Times* on Sunday. I may or may not be preggers and I know a garden or a patio is asking a lot 'for London' but I'd really love a view. Views are good for children, and for the soul. Don't you think?

Beat.

CASSANDRA: Congratulations, that's a big step, exciting step, the next exciting *(coughs)* chapter of your lives. Aren't you in for a real treat? I have for you today, brand spanking new to the market 'Western Gateway Two' located in the up-and-coming 'trendy' Stratford. Only half an hour from the hustle and bustle of Central London, with stupendous views of the Olympic park. Prices for two bedrooms start from around –

FREDDIE: *(Unseen.) What* is your problem?

CASSANDRA: I don't have a problem

FREDDIE: *(Unseen.)* Won't give me a mortgage? What is this, Nazi Germany? After all, I'm not representative of 'most of the population'.

CASSANDRA: Not following here.

FREDDIE: *(Unseen.)* I'm just your run-of-the-mill first-time buyer educated at the University of St Andrews with a second class degree in Geography and I'm having trouble taking out a mortgage. I'm having trouble applying for the Right to Buy scheme, I'm having trouble finding a job and in general I'm just having a lot of fucking trouble. Tell me the truth. Are all these units sold to *(whispers)* foreign investors?

CASSANDRA: Of course. You should be able to take out a mortgage. Although you won't be eligible for the Right to Buy scheme since you don't live in a council flat.

FREDDIE: *(Unseen.)* How would you know?

CASSANDRA: Sorry. D'you think we could pause for one second?

FREDDIE: *(Unseen.)* Try not to break protocol or the fourth wall Cassandra.

CASSANDRA: But you are comparing two realities which have no relation to one another!

Lights go up.

FREDDIE emerges.

FREDDIE: *There's* your mistake Sisi!

CASSANDRA: No mistake.

FREDDIE: Details, details.

CASSANDRA: *(Mumbling.)* I was simply picking apart your improbable scenario...

FREDDIE: Excuse me?

CASSANDRA: The scenario. It's ridiculous!

FREDDIE: No I understand. It *is* difficult. Not many hard-working and valued members of society earn an income of eighty to ninety grand a month. But I'll be sure to put you on the mailing list for future properties within your price range.

CASSANDRA: Though 'I wouldn't hold my breath'?

FREDDIE: Yes! Cut them off like you're cutting a piece of chorizo, saw through the fat and the garlic and do not, on any account tell them the truth.

CASSANDRA: What truth?

FREDDIE: The truth that we are saving these suckers for foreigners with cash to hand. Duh.

CASSANDRA: Prioritising foreign investment.

FREDDIE: Ding ding ding! You get the special prize!

CASSANDRA: This is unethical.

FREDDIE: Enlighten me.

CASSANDRA: You can't just reserve homes.

FREDDIE: Oh, Christ. Next you're going to erupt in some rhetoric along the lines of *(whining)* 'is a home simply a hollow shell for laundering cash? Do these Chinese investors even *like* London?'

CASSANDRA: You're not being serious.

FREDDIE: I'm the 'serious business' Sisi.

CASSANDRA: I don't believe it.

FREDDIE: Who needs belief when you've got capitalism darling!

CASSANDRA: You. Your methods. Wrong.

FREDDIE: We are making a difference. That's what you said in your interview. The Chinese are investing in our crumbling infrastructure.

CASSANDRA: I was...posturing.

FREDDIE: You did what you needed to do. Admirable. But this...this isn't you.

CASSANDRA: London is not a safety deposit box.

FREDDIE: You're right. London is the 'New Orient'. Though perhaps we'll go with something a little less dramatic with marketing. 'Xinhua Bu' I think would suit.

Beat.

You failed to impress the partners Sisi.

CASSANDRA: I don't care.

FREDDIE: You're breaking my heart here.

CASSANDRA: I don't care, I don't need this. I mean, I do but this is...too much. That was –

FREDDIE: We're giving you a second chance.

CASSANDRA: I'm not sleeping with you again.

FREDDIE: Good god, no. I've managed to convince them to let you accompany me to the final 'Invest in the West' exhibition dinner.

CASSANDRA: Tonight?

FREDDIE: You accept?

CASSANDRA: I don't know. I don't think so.

FREDDIE: Do you know what the starting salary for a Junior Associate at Avarita is Sisi?

Pause.

Good good good.

CASSANDRA: Who is the 'guest of honour'?

FREDDIE: Already thinking of the bigger picture.
Big shot investor. Chum of our CEO. Um. He's just bought a nuclear power plant in Sizewell. Sir...

CASSANDRA: Sir Alfred Lim?

FREDDIE: That's the one. Him and his cronies want a 'night out on the town' before signing on the dotted line. The 'Powers that Be' thought a female presence would be...

CASSANDRA: Chinks don't play better with cunt in the room.

FREDDIE: Bit of a stereotype Sisi. Self-possessed, seductive, submissive, you will undoubtedly contribute towards our success and smooth over those rough edges. *(Beat.)* By the way we've got a pool over what he'll build. If you want in.

CASSANDRA: Super-duper shopping outlet mall, cab factory, casino maybe.

FREDDIE: He bought London black cabs?

CASSANDRA: His competitor. Lim.

FREDDIE: Ha. Strange to think our taxis are now Chinese.

CASSANDRA: You do know they own our water supply?

FREDDIE: Yes.

CASSANDRA: The Chinese have a 8.68 per cent stake in Thames Water.

FREDDIE: Yes, I did know that *actually.*

CASSANDRA: And you do *not* want to piss off the guys who can piss in the water supply.

FREDDIE: Get excited Cassandra.

CASSANDRA: Fine.

FREDDIE: I didn't quite hear you.

CASSANDRA: Can hardly wait!

FREDDIE: Convincing you was easier than I thought.

CASSANDRA: I have a mortgage.

FREDDIE: Fair enough. Oh and remember –

CASSANDRA: Short and tight?

FREDDIE: Ha! Yes that, and remember Sisi, you are an estate agent. Scum of the earth.

He salutes her.

I'll pick you up around eight. See you later alligator.

He exits.

CASSANDRA: You won't survive.

BLACKOUT.

Transition to...

SCENE FOUR

Room. Flat. South South South London.

Lights up on CHARMAINE, who is pulling on her jumper, FRASER is buckling his belt – they continue dressing in awkward silence. CHARMAINE finds her mobile, begins texting.

He waves in front of her face obnoxiously. She continues to ignore him.

FRASER: I'd forgotten your 'enigmatic' nature. Keeps one on one's toes...

CHARMAINE: Part of my charm

FRASER: I feel old

CHARMAINE: You're not old.

FRASER: Do you regret –

CHARMAINE: No, no Fraser, course not. We had a great relationship. It simply ran its course.

   Pause.

FRASER: I actually meant just now but good to know

CHARMAINE: Oh. Right. Well. 'Just now' was bad judgement

FRASER: I wouldn't put a label on it

CHARMAINE: Won't happen again

FRASER: Why won't it happen again?

CHARMAINE: You *are* the limit Hamilton.

FRASER: What did you mean before, our relationship 'ran its course'?

CHARMAINE: Change the subject

FRASER: Sure, fine, OK.

Beat.

Though. Here I was thinking –

CHARMAINE: You think too much

FRASER: Our relationship ended because *you* couldn't commit

CHARMAINE: You've done something

FRASER: Nothing

CHARMAINE: You've got 'that' look

FRASER: People are always telling me I've got 'that look' face. Apologies.

CHARMAINE: I'm broke

FRASER: I wasn't going to ask for money!

CHARMAINE: If you say so

FRASER: Chip on my shoulder *actually*

CHARMAINE: Your parents are rich

FRASER: *Retired*

CHARMAINE: Why do you love acting like their privilege is your damage?

FRASER: Because they are the worst human beings in the world?

CHARMAINE: For supporting you, providing you with every opportunity...

FRASER: I couldn't breathe. Suffocating sycophants who believed everything can be worked towards, can be obtained through 'hard work'.

CHARMAINE: It's OK to fail Fraser.

FRASER: How did we get here?

CHARMAINE: You walked in unannounced wanting to reminisce about the 'good old days'.

FRASER: I want *you*

CHARMAINE: Where are you living?

FRASER: You care?

CHARMAINE: I only

FRASER: You *care.*

CHARMAINE: I was *only* being 'congenial'

FRASER: Admit you never wanted to buy a place

CHARMAINE: We would have been paying for it until we were seventy

FRASER: You were always crap at math Charmaine.

CHARMAINE: Mortgage alone

FRASER: Fact is, you didn't fancy being in debt to my parents!

CHARMAINE: Right. That's right. You are absolutely right. Hit the nail on the head. I didn't fancy being in debt to your parents.

FRASER: You hate them.

CHARMAINE: My mother worked really hard to support me.

FRASER: Gotcha. Avoid. Evade. Deny.

CHARMAINE: She worked herself to the point where...

FRASER: You work hard too.

CHARMAINE: We're having lunch right, and she blurts out: 'I used to work in a Chinese supermarket. It was hell'.

FRASER: We've all had jobs we'd rather repress...

CHARMAINE: Newly arrived in London. Barely any English. She was apparently terrible, messed up orders, stock lists were always going missing. Part of her job was to 'demonstrate' how to cook frozen dumplings for punters

FRASER: What was the shop called?

CHARMAINE: 'Loon Fung'. You could get anything from anywhere. Hawaiian t-shirts, fried chicken, fake Rolexes.

FRASER: *(Laughs.)* We need to go there *now*.

CHARMAINE: No longer exists.

FRASER: Demolished to make way for a state of the art bullshit, minimalist, designer coffee cart?

CHARMAINE: Crossrail.

FRASER: Shame.

CHARMAINE: My mother survived. She *survived*. Discrimination, abuse. But she had committed to this life. Became fluent, got a well-paid job. Met dad. Bought her flat eventually, and at a discount.

FRASER: Why are you telling me this?

CHARMAINE: Everyone blames the Right to Buy, Thatcher...

FRASER: *Well.*

CHARMAINE: Are they the ones to blame? Do you think my mum is to blame, your parents?

FRASER: For the housing crisis?

CHARMAINE: We can't afford to live in our city!

FRASER: 'Our city'?

CHARMAINE: Yes. Our city. Yours. Mine. Even wanker Andy's.

FRASER: What makes you think it's 'our city' Charmaine?

CHARMAINE: I don't think.

FRASER: You 'believe'!

CHARMAINE: Not funny.

FRASER: Not laughing. I understand what you're trying to say, that it's like we're not, that it's like, I don't know *(beat)* we don't belong here

CHARMAINE: *I* belong here.

FRASER: So who? Who is to blame for the 'housing crisis'?

CHARMAINE: I don't know, the Chinese.

FRASER: New plan. Let's storm the Chinese consulate and throw Red Books at 'em!

CHARMAINE: I didn't mean.

FRASER: What *did* you mean?

CHARMAINE: This is serious!

FRASER: Let's 'seriously' blame the Chinese for the reason why you didn't want to buy a flat

CHARMAINE: That is *not* what I am saying!

FRASER: You need to be more clear. Not one of your strong suits I know.

CHARMAINE: Tea. I need tea. Do you want tea?

FRASER: I'd rather a beer.

CHARMAINE: For the record. Don't despise your parents. Hardly know them.

FRASER: My fault too I suppose?

CHARMAINE: I'll get you your drink. *Highness.*

She curtsies, exits.

FRASER: She's right. *(Calling.)* You're right Charmaine. As per usual. Why should we have invested in our future?

BLACKOUT.

Transition to...

SCENE FIVE

Private dining room. Restaurant in Soho.

FREDDIE and CASSANDRA are seated in-between various Chinese businessmen (though unseen). They are now wearing evening attire.

Lights up on CASSANDRA and FREDDIE, holding champagne flutes, they raise them. Toast...

FREDDIE: Gom bui!

CASSANDRA: Gom bui!

They drink. CASSANDRA covers her mouth to hide a burp.

FREDDIE: Can't handle your 'Dom' Sisi?

He pours her more champagne.

Did you enjoy your 'bao yu' Sisi?

CASSANDRA: Very much

FREDDIE: Way to spoil a girl. Please do send the chef my Junior Associate's compliments! Ta Bu Hwei Shwa Guang Dong Hua *(She can't speak any Cantonese)*. You speak Cantonese don't you Sisi?

CASSANDRA: Afraid I never had any time for 'extra-curriculars'.

FREDDIE: Ah, yes you told me you *lived* in the library.

Beat.

As a matter of fact Sir Lim I spent my gap year in a village in Hunan province and on our first night they served Abalone with human breast milk. I know, I know but I must admit, despite the controversy, it was rather good *(Beat.)* Adventure? Yes, I'd say it *was* an adventure!

CASSANDRA: Each and every Eton boy needs his
The Beach moment.

FREDDIE: The villagers wouldn't stop poking fun at my
accent, they believed my Cantonese was far and
away more advanced than my Putonghua, 'Néih góng
matyéh wá?'

CASSANDRA: *(A bit too loudly.)* Would anyone like dessert?

FREDDIE: What can I say, I'm a roamer, wanderer,
wayfarer, nomad, I love travelling. It's a drug.
Seven Years in Tibet? Favourite film. Not that...aha,
no... I mean obviously Tibet *is* China. Tibet belongs to
China. I am a firm believer in that Tibet, Taiwan, Hong
Kong and Singapore rightfully belong to China.

CASSANDRA: How many for Port?

FREDDIE: I went to Oxford too, yes. Classics. *(Beat.)*
Oh, ya, Meadow. Gorgeous. Spent many of a,
'you know' *(laughs)* you know! I was in the squad.
Novices. You too? Bloody Cambridge *(beat)* crucified us.
Do you row Sisi?

CASSANDRA: I don't row I'm afraid, no.

FREDDIE: Britain is like, a what? An 'island of ghosts'?
I agree with you Mr. Tung. Of course I agree with
you. But it is still Great Britain. Look at the great
opportunities for investment, industry, transport,
technology, and of course – *property.*

CASSANDRA: You sound like a 'Great Britain' advertisement
Freddie!

FREDDIE: *(Laughs.)* Have you heard these slogans? /
They're AWESOME.

CASSANDRA: Perhaps later / at the club! Speaking of we
should be going –

He claps his hands together.

FREDDIE: Great great great. *(Muttering.)* She loves a bit of roleplay, our Sisi. *(Normal.)* Culture is...?

CASSANDRA: *Not playing*

FREDDIE: *(Aside.) Oh come now Sisi, you started this. Besides your job is hanging by a fucking thread (To the room.) Culture is...?*

She takes a long swig of champers.

CASSANDRA: *(Deadpan.)* Culture is great.

FREDDIE: Innovation is?

CASSANDRA: Great.

FREDDIE: More enthusiasm, please. Shopping is...?

CASSANDRA: Great!

FREDDIE: Better. Heritage?

CASSANDRA: Is great!

FREDDIE: Innovation?

CASSANDRA: Is great!

FREDDIE: Knowledge?

CASSANDRA: Great!

FREDDIE: Technology? Is great! I've got one. I've a really good one. Self-deprecating humour?

Beat.

Is great!

He laughs.

Your turn Sisi!

Beat.

CASSANDRA: Um. Shakespeare...

FREDDIE: Is great!

CASSANDRA: Fish and chips...

FREDDIE: Is great!

Beat.

CASSANDRA: Binge drinking *(Beat.)* Binge drinking...is great!

FREDDIE: I'm sure everyone has heard enough

CASSANDRA: BREXIT...is great!

FREDDIE: Stop

CASSANDRA: Unaffordable housing

FREDDIE: Cassandra

CASSANDRA: Is great! Bombing Syria

FREDDIE: Stop it / stop it now

CASSANDRA: Is great! Tax-avoiding Tories

FREDDIE: You're not funny

CASSANDRA: Are the greatest.

She gets more and more carried away...

Rampant illiteracy, third runway at Heathrow, attacks against homosexuals, Islamic faith, women, the working class, 'THE EMPIRE'! Lastly, though in no way the least –

FREDDIE: *(Pleading.)* Compassion, freedom of speech, democracy. Sit / down.

CASSANDRA: The inability to admit defeat...IS GREAT!

FREDDIE: Enough!

She sits down.

CASSANDRA: Welcome to the New Orient.

FREDDIE: *(To CASSANDRA.)* Bitch.

He drinks his own and her glass.

Just look at that silver spoon dangling out of that beautiful mouth...

CASSANDRA: 'When will my reflection show who I am inside?'

FREDDIE: Don't mess this up for me or else –

CASSANDRA: Or else you'll serve up my balls on a platter of Peking duck? You're beginning to sound like a broken record Fred.

FREDDIE: This isn't over.

CASSANDRA: You're drunk.

FREDDIE: Why? I helped you.

CASSANDRA: Roads, buildings, fields. Stitched together through time. Abandoned, plagued, burned, yet it survives. This city. How it began. Beautiful chaos. Where Roman merchants once saw a port in a ditch...

FREDDIE: What the fuck?

CASSANDRA: Tonight it ends.

FREDDIE: I invested in you.

She begins to stand.

FREDDIE pushes her back down.

Gentlemen. I, Freddie Reynolds, would like to say a few words...

BLACKOUT.

Transition to...

SCENE SIX

Room. Flat. South South South London.

CHARMAINE re-enters with two beers. She gives FRASER one.

CHARMAINE: Misery loves company.

FRASER: Let's toast

She lifts her glass.

Here's to failed reunions! Cheers.

They drink.

FRASER: I've been trying to figure out

CHARMAINE: *Why* you've returned to Chez Car Crash

FRASER: To check in

CHARMAINE: You needn't have bothered

FRASER: Because *you* think I never 'bothered' when we were together?

CHARMAINE: You were numb most of the time, how on earth could you remember most of 'when we were together'? Three years worth of you loafing, using me, using –

FRASER: Not fair

CHARMAINE: What, the cool kids don't smoke the reefer no more?

FRASER: Why are you being such a bitch? *(Beat.)* Could we draw truce for a second?

Beat.

Broken record.

CHARMAINE: Yeah we are a broken record.

FRASER: Truth is, you –

CHARMAINE: I'm moving back home

FRASER: Your mum never mentioned

CHARMAINE: I'm almost thirty, and I'm moving back in with my mother. I mean I can't, I can't keep doing this. Packing up, moving on, packing up, moving on –

FRASER: You love it. You've moved more than seven times in the past three years.

CHARMAINE: Can't be seven.

FRASER: Hammersmith was sixth.

CHARMAINE: Haringey seventh.

FRASER: We never left the house.

CHARMAINE: Best Turkish food in the city.

FRASER: *(Laughs.)* Best Turkish food?

CHARMAINE: Before. I'm sorry.

FRASER: I was being a dick.

CHARMAINE: I have trouble –

FRASER: Living in the present?

CHARMAINE: Fuck you Fraser!

FRASER: You still don't want kids?

CHARMAINE: Can we just sit and drink?

FRASER: You once said you didn't want what everybody else had. We weren't going to be like 'everyone else'.

CHARMAINE: *(Rising.) I just didn't want to buy a place, OK?*

FRASER: I didn't just want to buy a place. I wanted to buy a place with you!

CHARMAINE: You want the truth? OK. You want the fucking truth? I didn't want to buy a place with you.

Pause.

Say something.

FRASER: *I bought the flat*

CHARMAINE: No

FRASER: I bought the flat in East London.

CHARMAINE: No

FRASER: I bought it *for you*!

CHARMAINE: I never bloody asked for it!

FRASER: It's an investment Charmaine.

CHARMAINE: It will be a prison!

FRASER: I'll go, I should go. I'll go.

CHARMAINE: You better go

FRASER: Change your mind

CHARMAINE: Too late

FRASER: We're a bit like London

CHARMAINE: You are the only man I know who has the ability to construct pseudo-metaphors on-demand!

FRASER: But here we are building brick by brick. Investing *(beat)* in a life. Risking –

CHARMAINE: The risk was too high.

FRASER: Alright then.

Pause.

Could you *(beat)* lie to me?

Beat.

CHARMAINE: I have...packing to do Fraser. You need to leave.

FRASER: Won't bother asking you to stay in touch 'cause you probably won't

CHARMAINE: Probably!

FRASER: Every conversation, argument, touch, caress, every *fuck* became about *this*. This idea, concept, dream, it consumed us. Home, a home, our home. 'Home is where the heart is', that's what they say isn't it?

CHARMAINE: Don't forget *that*.

She points to his shopping. He grabs it and walks over to the door.

FRASER: Change your mind.

BLACKOUT.

Transition to...

<u>SCENE SEVEN</u>

Restaurant. Soho.

Lights go up on the mess of a dining room (we can assume the businessmen have left...embarrassed).

FREDDIE is on the floor. He's just thrown up. He wipes his mouth.

CASSANDRA enters. She stares at the mess, and FREDDIE.

FREDDIE: Know what you're about to say – *don't.*

FREDDIE begins picking up bottles to see if they're empty. He finds one.

What did you put in my drink?

CASSANDRA: Give it me.

FREDDIE: I deserve this.

He drinks again.

CASSANDRA: You've had more than enough.

He belches loudly.

FREDDIE: Bet you're *pleased* with yourself. Pleased, pleased pleased.

CASSANDRA: Do you need me to call you an Uber?

FREDDIE: Congratulations! Your plan to destroy me –

CASSANDRA: Oh, you screwed this up without any of *my* help.

FREDDIE: What did you say to them?

CASSANDRA: Who?

FREDDIE: The Chinese fuckers. Did you explain –

CASSANDRA: Well. They moved on from the shock they sustained from your antics earlier, eventually.

Although I had a bloody whale of a time explaining why you acted like a petulant child before disappearing off into the neon-lit smoke-filled corridor. And they were disappointed that you didn't accompany us to the club.

Pause.

FREDDIE: Don't tell me you got that old decrepit bald one to stand up and give a half-decent rendition of 'My Girl'?

CASSANDRA: I'm half Chinese. I kill at karaoke. Oh and he was more of an Elton John fan: 'I'm Still Standing'.

FREDDIE: In answer to your incessantly pointless irrelevant exhaustive rhetoric yes I *know* I made a fool of myself.

CASSANDRA: Good to know.

She takes out her phone and begins secretly recording his drunken tirade...

FREDDIE: You mumble.

CASSANDRA: *(Calmly.)* I do *not* mumble

FREDDIE: You talk chatter speak spit mumble incoherently consistently out of the *side of your mouth.* It's like listening to Gary Sinise fuck Bruce Springsteen in a hot tub full of bankers loaded on MDMA and Schnapps!

CASSANDRA: What does that even mean?

FREDDIE: We should really work on real estate jargon. It's just so bitter and cold and unfeeling don't you think? Where's the 'fun'?

CASSANDRA: We are estate agents, 'scum of the earth'. You should get yourself home.

FREDDIE: I have no home!

CASSANDRA: Come on.

FREDDIE: *This* is my home!

CASSANDRA: Try getting up.

FREDDIE: I've been in this business ten years. TEN YEARS. What do you think they thought of my performance? Want my opinion? FUCKING GOLDEN.

CASSANDRA: Yes I think they definitely experienced the full force of your 'performance'.

FREDDIE: Saboteur.

CASSANDRA: I give up.

She turns off her mobile's camera.

FREDDIE: Ten fucking years.

She turns around.

Do not walk away from me or I will report you, your constant diatribes, blatant racism, general lack of functionality, human decency...

CASSANDRA: Aha! Ding-dong, the bastard's not dead. Do you think I give two pence about this job?

FREDDIE: I am Freddie Reynolds, the face of *Avarita Global International Worldwide Properties Limited* and as the face of *Avarita Global International Worldwide Properties Limited* I hold responsibility to not only my clients but to my company and their employees. You will not leave this room without my permission!

CASSANDRA: Do you even hear yourself?

FREDDIE: Wait, wait. Please wait. Sisi. Cassandra. I don't want to be alone. Please. Just. Sit with me for a while and then I'll go home and I'll never bother you again. I promise.

He begins to sober up.

CASSANDRA: Five minutes.

FREDDIE: I fucked this up.

CASSANDRA: You did threaten an entire room of very wealthy, very influential, probably very dangerous businessmen and senior members of the Communist Party that unless they invested in 'Western Gateway I' and 'Western Gateway II' you'd see to it that the opposing Middle Eastern buyers would not only be given a discount and lower interest rate, but they'd be served their competitor's mother's cunts as an appetizer at the closing deal ceremony.

FREDDIE: I don't remember.

CASSANDRA: But y'know, who am I to say they would consider that an insult?

FREDDIE: But what he asked before, what's so 'great' about Great Britain...

CASSANDRA: Come on Fred.

FREDDIE: He was right. What's the fucking point? There's nothing 'great' about it. Nothing attractive for the oligarch.

CASSANDRA: Things. Many, many things.

FREDDIE: Go on then. But you're not allowed 'freedom of speech'.

CASSANDRA: The Queen *(beat)* Wills and Kate. Fish and chips. Red postboxes. Jamie Oliver. Harry Potter. Tax-free shopping. Not forgetting. Premier League clubs and Yorkshire villages. Boris bus, Boris bikes, *BORIS*. The Thames, though no longer British per se. I'd say that was a pretty 'attractive' list?

FREDDIE: Lists of things don't make an identity, a country, define a culture...

CASSANDRA: Rest of the world begs to differ

FREDDIE: What you said back at the restaurant: binge drinking. Self-deprecating humour. Bombing Syria. Tax-dodging Tories. Inability to admit defeat. *Epiphany...*

CASSANDRA: And I do so pity you Freddie Reynolds.

FREDDIE: Epiphany. I've had an epiphany

CASSANDRA: OK so you've 'had an epiphany'.

FREDDIE: London is not a safety deposit box. It's a place. It's got a heartbeat, full of people, real people, from the genius to the misunderstood and I know I'm not making any sense but you understand. I'm going to change my life.

CASSANDRA: You should really speak to someone.

FREDDIE: *(Laughs gently.)* But I have you.

He attempts to kiss her. She moves away.

All they're doing is driving the price of property up and up. Unaffordable palaces that no one wants to live in.

CASSANDRA: And you're telling me you had no idea?

FREDDIE: They don't care, they just don't fucking care. THEY'RE ONLY HERE TO BUY SOY SAUCE.

CASSANDRA: What are you going on about, 'soy sauce'?

FREDDIE: You know the urban legend don't you? Some Canto pop star shits get heavy into a sex scandal. Chinese TV, stuck in the fucking '80s, goes out onto the cold and lonely city streets to get the people's verdict. They want to find the real. And boy do they find it. Some middle-aged geezer holding two shopping bags filled with cabbages, 'for dinner' he says. So they ask what he thinks about the Canto pop star shits' immorality and they wait for the deplorable reprimand he will no doubt give to their viewers, to their pathetic little TV spot. But what does he say in response? Cassandra. What does he say?

CASSANDRA: No clue.

Beat.

FREDDIE: *I'm Just Here to Buy Soy Sauce!*

He begins laughing.

That's what he said. Get it? I'm just a real guy who doesn't give a fuck about anything. I'm here minding my own business. He went viral. Weibo netizens ate it right the fuck up. It's now a thing, you know, a phrase you use when you don't want to get your hands dirty. Isn't that something?

Pause.

CASSANDRA: I single-handedly steered this sinking ship.

FREDDIE: *(Muttering.)* I'm not feeling too good.

CASSANDRA: You lost your firm a billion-pound deal because of a moral epiphany. Soy sauce? I mean. Will you ever stop with the generalisations. Fucking racist.

FREDDIE: What this city will become!

CASSANDRA: Benefits everybody.

FREDDIE: Hollow empty shells.

CASSANDRA: That phrase sums up the deal rather nicely though. I mean, who really gives a shit about any of it, because, aren't we all just 'here to buy soy sauce'?

Beat. Her phone beeps.

FREDDIE: People need places to live. Real places to live, homes, not two-thousand foot phallic obelisks with 'panoramic views' of the Olympic park. Cassandra. You were right. About all of it. But we can do something. Will you, will you join me in making the world a better place? Leave Avarita behind and –

CASSANDRA bursts into laughter...tears...

CASSANDRA: Oh my god. This is...

Beat.

This is one merry-go-round too many.

Her mobile beeps.

That's my Uber.

FREDDIE: Together we can make a difference! We can expose the truth!

CASSANDRA: How would that work exactly?

FREDDIE: There's blood on your hands.

CASSANDRA: Fun as this has been...

FREDDIE: Please, Cassandra!

He attempts to restrain her. She slaps his face.

CASSANDRA: STOP!

Pause.

I'm sorry. This was the only way.

He says nothing.

Freddie? I'm waving the white flag. Armistice. Cease fire. Truce. Whatever you want to call it.

FREDDIE: Expand.

CASSANDRA: I won't reveal the truth...

She taps her mobile.

FREDDIE: You won't publicly humiliate me if I recommend you for the job

CASSANDRA: *Your* job to be precise *and* that we never meet again.

Silence.

Put in for a transfer Fred. Or leave. I don't care.

FREDDIE: I care about this city. I'm not just...

CASSANDRA: We all have to make a living.

FREDDIE: I'm not just here to buy soy sauce.

CASSANDRA: Onwards and upwards.

She exhales loudly.

I've just made the biggest sale of property in British history.

She exits.

FREDDIE closes his eyes.

Stands.

Moves centre stage...

EPILOGUE

Spotlight on FREDDIE.

He taps the Mic a couple times.

FREDDIE: Ahlan! Vaazhga! Yokoso! Selamat datang! Dobro pazálovat! Huan ying ni, *welcome* to the official launch of 'Third World Gateway I' and 'Third World Gateway II', part of *Avarita Global Worldwide International Properties Limited* awe-inspiring, ground-breaking, DPRK, UN, Amnesty International sanctioned global initiative 'Invest in the Third World!'

Spotlight on CHARMAINE, who begins to pack, she reads off the receipt/poem.

CHARMAINE: Agents huddle, step gingerly over puddles...

FREDDIE: *Welcome* to the official launch of 'Third World Gateway I' and 'Third World Gateway II', part of *Avarita*

Global Worldwide International Properties Limited awe-inspiring, ground-breaking, DPRK, UN, Amnesty International sanctioned global initiative 'Invest in the Third World!'

CHARMAINE: Glossy catalogues tucked beneath elbows, Savile Row blinks in the harsh unreflective surface of concrete, derelict walls that cry 'no entry'.

FREDDIE: The world's changed quite a bit in the last five years but *Avarita* is right there alongside it, consistently *and* persistently challenging those boring old Western sensibilities!

CHARMAINE: Olympian tragedy, hotel suicide, Mao en Vogue

FREDDIE: We're offering not 'a' but the 'the' unique project.

CHARMAINE: Shivering beneath the surface, the ancient ferocity of ages, recognition, a slap, cheek on, appearances are everything

FREDDIE: We are a Beacon for the East – looking West!

CHARMAINE: Icarus in Stratford.

FREDDIE: I'm Freddie Reynolds, Junior Associate here at *Avarita's* China HQ in Shanghai

CHARMAINE: I dream about him all the time.

FREDDIE: And it is with the *greatest* pleasure to be speaking to you this afternoon all the way from the *greatest* city in the world!

She tears it up.

So *what* are you waiting for?

CHARMAINE: Maybe if I just close my eyes.

FREDDIE: Invest in the Third World today!

THE END.

Jingan Young is an award-winning playwright. She holds a BA (Hons) in English with Film Studies from King's College London and a Master of Studies in Creative Writing from the University of Oxford. She is currently reading for a PhD in Film Studies at King's College London. She was the first playwright commissioned and produced in the English language by the Hong Kong Arts Festival for FILTH (Failed in London, Try Hong Kong). In 2016, she was a member of the BBC's Writers Room invitation only group London Voices. She was acknowledged for her screenwriting by the BBC and Idris Elba on the New Talent Hotlist 2017. She is founder and artistic director of POKFULAM RD PRODUCTIONS 薄扶林道© and regularly commissions new writing from East Asian writers in the UK and China.

WWW.OBERONBOOKS.COM